TRANSFORMING SCOTLAND

*A Barna Report
produced in partnership with
the Maclellan Foundation*

Transforming Scotland © 2015 by Barna Group. All rights reserved.
ISBN 978-0-9965843-0-2

All information contained in this document is copyrighted by Barna Group and shall remain the property of Barna Group. U.S.A. and international copyright laws protect the contents of this document in their entirety. Any reproduction, modification, distribution, transmission, publication, translation, display, hosting or sale of all or any portion of the contents of this document is strictly prohibited without written permission of an authorised representative of Barna Group.

The information contained in this report is true and accurate to the best knowledge of the copyright holder. It is provided without warranty of any kind: express, implied or otherwise. In no event shall Barna Group, Barna Research, or employees of Barna Group be liable for any special, incidental, indirect or consequential damages of any kind, or any damages whatsoever resulting from the use of this information, whether or not users have been advised of the possibility of damage, or on any theory of liability, arising out of or in connection with the use of this information.

CONTENTS

INTRODUCTION	04
PART I. THE STATE OF FAITH IN SCOTLAND	12
PART II. BEST PRACTICES FOR TRANSFORMATIVE MINISTRY	38
1. Leader Training & Empowerment	40
2. Leader Effectiveness & Accountability	42
3. Church Community	44
4. The Bible	47
5. Evangelism & Outreach	50
6. Serving & Social Justice	51
7. Prayer & Worship	54
8. Theology & Religious Activity	58
9. Stewardship & Vocation	60
10. Resources & Partnerships	62
PART III. MILLENNIALS STUDY	66
PART IV. IMPLICATIONS & RECOMMENDATIONS	76
APPENDICES	85
A. Data Tables, National Study	85
B. Data Tables, Best Practices Study	135
C. Bibliography of Secondary Research	165
D. Methodologies	169
E. Acknowledgements	174
ABOUT BARNA	175

THE STATE OF FAITH IN SCOTLAND

CHRISTIANITY

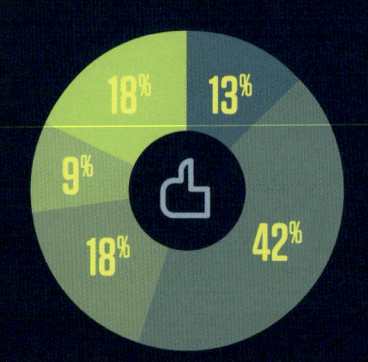

OVERALL, SCOTS HAVE A FAVOURABLE IMPRESSION OF CHRISTIANITY

- VERY FAVOURABLE — 13%
- FAIRLY FAVOURABLE — 42%
- FAIRLY UNFAVOURABLE — 18%
- VERY UNFAVOURABLE — 9%
- DON'T KNOW — 18%

YET, IN THE END, MOST SCOTS SAY RELIGIOUS FAITH HAS HAD A FAIRLY NEUTRAL EFFECT ON THEIR LIFE

- A NEGATIVE IMPACT — 2%
- HASN'T MADE MUCH OF A DIFFERENCE — 46%
- HELPFUL BUT NOT TRANSFORMATIVE — 36%
- GREATLY TRANSFORMED ME — 16%

PRESENT-DAY CHRISTIANITY IN SCOTLAND …

Legend:
- VERY ACCURATELY
- FAIRLY ACCURATELY
- NOT TOO ACCURATELY
- NOT AT ALL ACCURATELY
- DON'T KNOW

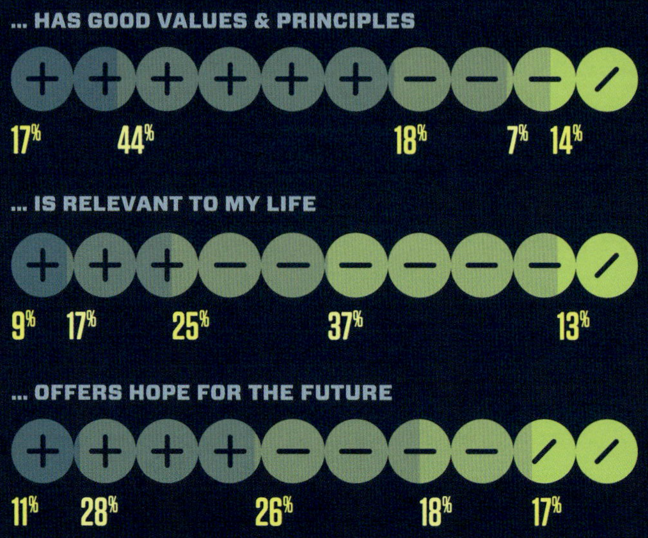

… HAS GOOD VALUES & PRINCIPLES
17% / 44% / 18% / 7% / 14%

… IS RELEVANT TO MY LIFE
9% / 17% / 25% / 37% / 13%

… OFFERS HOPE FOR THE FUTURE
11% / 28% / 26% / 18% / 17%

THE CHURCH

THE LAST TIME I WENT TO CHURCH WAS...

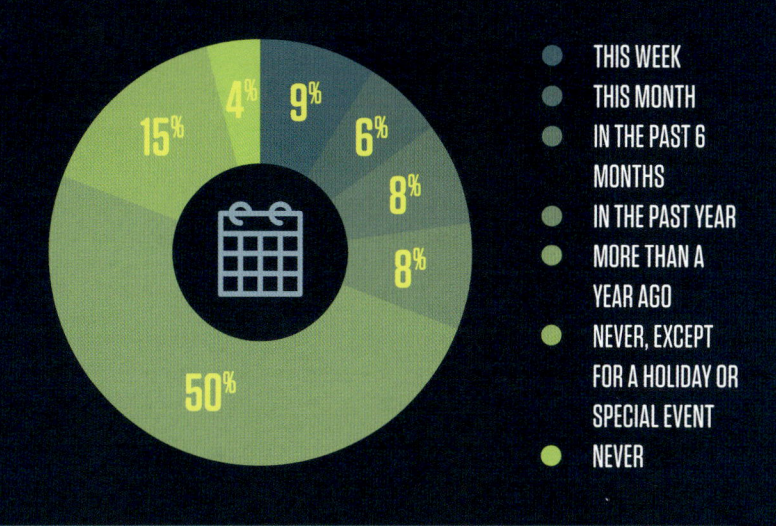

- 9% THIS WEEK
- 6% THIS MONTH
- 8% IN THE PAST 6 MONTHS
- 8% IN THE PAST YEAR
- 15% MORE THAN A YEAR AGO
- 4% NEVER, EXCEPT FOR A HOLIDAY OR SPECIAL EVENT
- 50% NEVER

TOP TWO REASONS SCOTS GIVE FOR NOT ATTENDING CHURCH

- I AM JUST NOT INTERESTED IN RELIGION — 70%
- THE CHURCH REALLY DOES NOT HAVE ANYTHING TO OFFER ME — 61%

TOP TWO REASONS FOR ATTENDING CHURCH WHICH SCOTS FIND MOST CONVINCING

- 50% TO MEET OTHER PEOPLE FROM THE COMMUNITY
- 32% TO FIND OUT MORE ABOUT GOD

THE STATE OF FAITH IN SCOTLAND

THE BIBLE

- **41%** BOOK OF TEACHINGS WRITTEN BY MEN
- **16%** NOT INSPIRED BY GOD, BUT TELLS HOW THE WRITERS UNDERSTOOD THE WAYS AND PRINCIPLES OF GOD
- **16%** INSPIRED WORD OF GOD BUT HAS SOME FACTUAL OR HISTORICAL ERRORS
- **10%** INSPIRED WORD OF GOD WITH NO ERRORS, BUT SOME VERSES ARE SYMBOLIC, NOT LITERAL
- **3%** ACTUAL WORD OF GOD AND SHOULD BE TAKEN LITERALLY, WORD FOR WORD
- **12%** I DON'T KNOW
- **3%** PREFER NOT TO ANSWER

LESS THAN THREE IN 10 SCOTS BELIEVE THE BIBLE IS THE ACTUAL OR INSPIRED WORD OF GOD

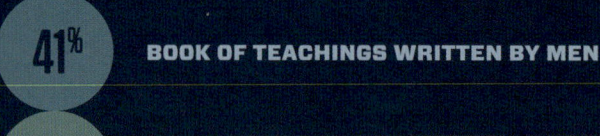

THE BIBLE IS TOTALLY ACCURATE IN ALL OF THE PRINCIPLES IT TEACHES

5%	11%	28%	42%	14%
STRONGLY AGREE	TEND TO AGREE	TEND TO DISAGREE	STRONGLY DISAGREE	DON'T KNOW

NEARLY 9 IN 10 SCOTS ARE NEUTRAL (44%) OR SCEPTICAL (42%) TOWARDS THE BIBLE

NEUTRAL: RARELY READ THE BIBLE AND ARE INDIFFERENT TOWARDS ITS AUTHORITY
SCEPTICAL: HOLD NEGATIVE ATTITUDES TOWARDS THE BIBLE

- **63%** OF SCOTS NEVER READ THE BIBLE
- **17%** DO SO LESS THAN ONCE A YEAR
- **10%** READ THE BIBLE 1-4 TIMES A YEAR
- **3%** READ IT ONCE A MONTH
- **4%** READ IT 1-3 TIMES A WEEK
- **1%** READ IT 4+ TIMES A WEEK
- **2%** READ THE BIBLE EVERY DAY

SCOTS SAY THE FOLLOWING WORDS OR PHRASES MOST ACCURATELY DESCRIBE HOW THEY SEE JESUS

- **37%** A PERSON WHO ACTUALLY LIVED, BUT WAS JUST A MORAL TEACHER OR PROPHET AND NOT GOD
- **24%** MADE TO BE THE 'SON OF GOD' BY HIS FOLLOWERS AFTER HIS DEATH
- **22%** IS MOST CONCERNED WITH MORALITY AND DOING GOOD
- **13%** SPEAKS TO YOU IN A WAY THAT IS RELEVANT TO YOUR LIFE
- **12%** IS GOD
- **12%** HIS FOLLOWERS ARE NOT GOOD EXAMPLES OF HIS TEACHINGS
- **10%** HEALS PEOPLE TODAY
- **8%** HAS DEEPLY TRANSFORMED YOUR LIFE
- **8%** IS ACTUALLY RETURNING TO EARTH AGAIN
- **13%** DON'T KNOW

INTRODUCTION

INTRODUCTION

What is the current state of Christianity, faith and the church in Scotland? Is spiritual transformation possible? What kinds of ministry and mission are working to transform people, families and communities with the gospel? Are there signs of life and growth, even as overall church attendance is at an all-time low? Where do we find ministry initiatives with the greatest potential to transform lives, and can we identify common themes among transformative ministries? If so, can we adapt these themes to different contexts—urban, rural, young, old, poor, middle class—so that the country is transformed by the gospel?

To answer these questions, Barna Global, the international partner of Barna Group in California, USA, undertook a multi-phase research project. The first phase was a comprehensive review of previous research, including studies conducted by Tearfund, Christian Research and Peter Brierley, among others. (For a bibliography of secondary research, see Appendix C of this report.) This review informed Barna's approach in two crucial respects: 1) It set a vivid backdrop for an accurate sketch of the state of Christianity in Scotland, and 2) ensured Barna's research would break new ground, rather than channelling valuable resources to find what had already been discovered.

The second phase was a series of 29 in-depth interviews with key Christian leaders identified by the Transforming Scotland Steering Group. Although these leaders come from a breadth of theological and denominational backgrounds, an array of geographies and widely varying churches, ministries, businesses and political affiliations, consistent themes emerged from their interviews. For example, all the leaders agree, without exception, that spiritual transformation in Scotland is possible. While not every leader agrees on all the necessary catalysts, a majority concurs on the essential components of change (examined at length in this report). The interviews and their common themes informed the design of the final phase of research: a study of ministry best practices to find out what is working in Scotland and why.

Concurrent with the in-depth interviews were two national surveys: one of more than a thousand Scottish adults ages 18 and older, and another of 200 ministers/pastors of Protestant churches in Scotland. The two national surveys contained a handful of the same or similar questions to enable comparison and contrast of views. However, the study of the general population focused on assessing respondents' impressions of Christianity, personal experiences with church and faith, perceptions of churches and opinions of Jesus and the Bible. The minister/pastor survey, meanwhile, focused on ministry priorities and effectiveness, perceived barriers to more fruitful ministry and views of particular challenges facing the church in Scotland.

The final phase of research consisted of three studies to uncover a set of best ministry and mission practices. The first two studies were conducted December 2014 to January 2015 among a small cohort of Protestant evangelical churches identified by the Steering Group as either 'baseline' or 'growing'. Baseline churches represent the norm among evangelical churches in Scotland, acting as the 'control group' for the comparison study. Many are spiritually rich churches that are faithfully living out the gospel in their local community, yet they are experiencing limited numerical growth. Growing churches, meanwhile, stand out from the norm, reporting significant levels of growth. Because spiritual transformation is a difficult reality to measure, numerical growth—specifically, conversion growth, rather than transfer growth—is a quantitative proxy measurement that often indicates transformative ministry. Baseline and growing churches, and their leaders, responded to identical surveys about their beliefs, perspectives and behaviours—thus enabling parallel comparison to identify which factors, if any, stand out as indicators of transformational growth in these congregations.

During the same timeframe, Barna also interviewed a small cohort of faith-engaged Millennial Scots to discover their perspectives and experiences of church and faith. What 'best practices', if any, had their church communities adopted that motivated them to stay connected when so many adults of all ages are disengaging from church involvement? What factors are at work to help them live transformed lives, against the cultural tide? (See Part III for an overview of the findings from this study.)

The remainder of this report contains an overview of each phase of research, summary analysis of the findings and recommended 'next steps' for Transforming Scotland to invest in, support and initiate spiritual transformation across the nation.

SCOTLAND IS ...

A CHRISTIAN NATION

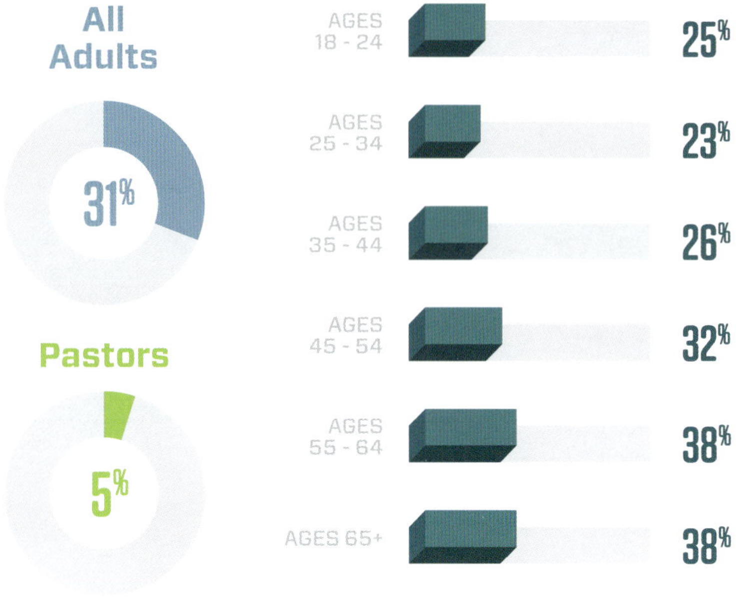

All Adults: 31%

Pastors: 5%

Age	Percentage
AGES 18 - 24	25%
AGES 25 - 34	23%
AGES 35 - 44	26%
AGES 45 - 54	32%
AGES 55 - 64	38%
AGES 65+	38%

A POST-CHRISTIAN NATION

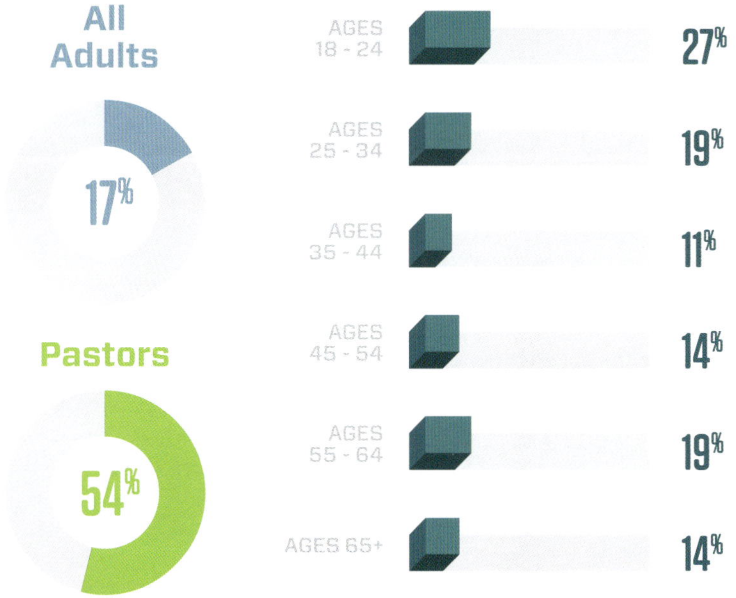

All Adults: 17%

Pastors: 54%

Age	Percentage
AGES 18 - 24	27%
AGES 25 - 34	19%
AGES 35 - 44	11%
AGES 45 - 54	14%
AGES 55 - 64	19%
AGES 65+	14%

A SECULAR NATION

All Adults: 19%

Pastors: 24%

Age	%
AGES 18 - 24	22%
AGES 25 - 34	22%
AGES 35 - 44	18%
AGES 45 - 54	19%
AGES 55 - 64	22%
AGES 65+	15%

A NATION IN SPIRITUAL TRANSITION

All Adults: 15%

Pastors: 41%

Age	%
AGES 18 - 24	14%
AGES 25 - 34	16%
AGES 35 - 44	14%
AGES 45 - 54	15%
AGES 55 - 64	9%
AGES 65+	21%

PART I
THE STATE OF FAITH IN SCOTLAND

Three out of 10 Scottish adults say 'a Christian nation' is the most accurate description of Scotland (31%). Taken on its own, that description is most popular—but a combined majority of Scots agrees with another option (51%): 'a secular nation' (19%), 'a post-Christian nation' (17%) and 'a nation in transition spiritually' (15%).

Given that a combined seven in 10 Scots have not attended a worship service in the past year (50%), have never been to church except for a special occasion (15%) or have never attended a Christian service of any kind (4%), those who chose 'a Christian nation'—who are more likely to be 55 or older—may share a concept of 'Christian' informed more by Scotland's cultural heritage than by a biblical understanding of following the Way of Jesus. This focus on cultural legacy is reasonable considering Scotland's rich Christian history, which can be traced to the fourth century or even earlier.

A NATION DIVIDED

- SELF-IDENTIFIED CHRISTIAN
- ANOTHER FAITH OR NO FAITH

51%

49%

17% Scots who say they have accepted Jesus as Saviour and made a personal commitment to him that is still important in their life today

% AMONG SELF-IDENTIFIED CHRISTIANS

- 5%
- 26%
- 69%

- **LEGACY CHRISTIANS**
  Self-identified Christians who do not believe basic elements of Christian doctrine or express personal faith in Jesus

- **NON-EVANGELICAL BORN AGAIN CHRISTIANS**
  Self-identified Christians who do not meet all of the qualifications of the Bebbington rubric, but who have accepted Jesus as Saviour and made a personal commitment to him that is still important in their life today

- **EVANGELICAL CHRISTIANS**
  Defined according to the Bebbington rubric; this category includes those who meet four qualifying standards—they perceive the Bible as totally accurate in all its teachings, have confessed their sins and accepted Jesus Christ as their Saviour, believe they have a responsibility to share their faith with others, and believe a conversion to Christianity is imperative for every person

CHRISTIAN BELIEF & PRACTICE

Scotland is a nation divided. Half of all Scots describe themselves as Christian (51%) while the other half identify with another faith or none (49%). The cultural trend to identify as Christian is in decline, as the trendline on the following chart demonstrates. Younger adults are much less apt than older adults to describe themselves as Christian.

RELIGIOUS SELF-IDENTIFICATION
% AMONG ALL ADULTS, BY AGE GROUP

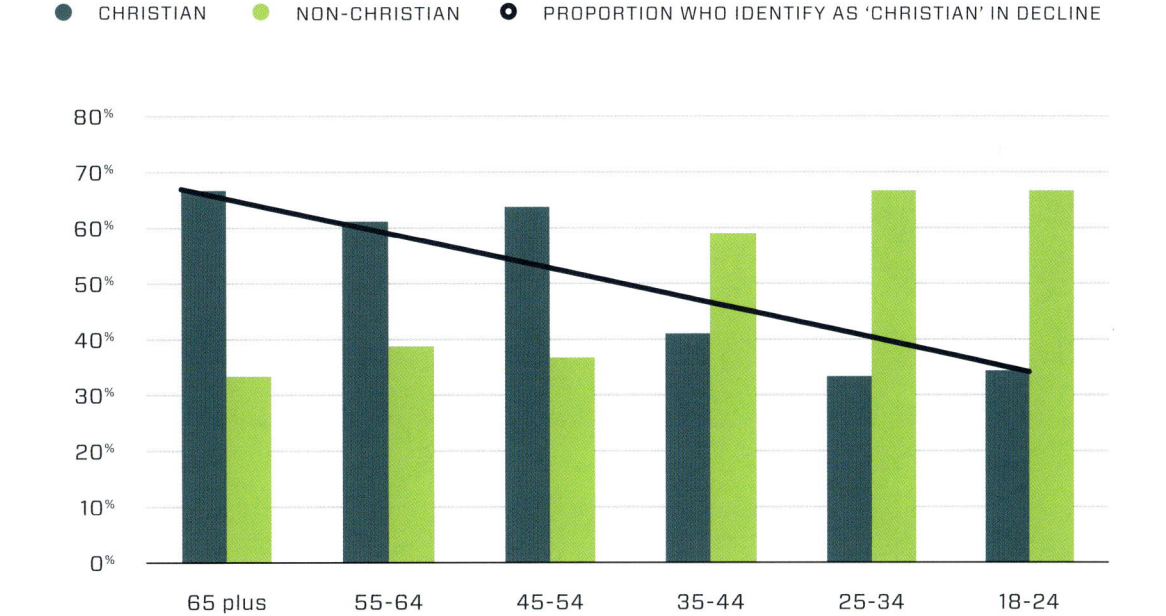

● CHRISTIAN   ● NON-CHRISTIAN   ○ PROPORTION WHO IDENTIFY AS 'CHRISTIAN' IN DECLINE

Age group	Christian	Non-Christian
65 plus	67%	33%
55-64	61%	39%
45-54	64%	37%
35-44	41%	59%
25-34	33%	67%
18-24	35%	67%

Christian Belief

Not all people who self-identify as Christian are fully engaged with or committed to their faith. For many, in fact, the label alone is enough. The power of Christendom's cultural legacy remains strong in Scotland, especially among older adults. This study found that seven out of 10 self-identified Christians are 'legacy Christians' who do not believe basic elements of Christian doctrine or express personal faith in Jesus (69%). This translates to more than one-third of the total population (36%). Interestingly, a legacy Christian is more likely than the average Scot to say 'a Christian nation' is the best way to describe the country (44% vs. 31%), a view which also demonstrates a more cultural than personally transformational view of their religious affiliation.

WHAT SCOTLAND BELIEVES
% of all adults

● STRONGLY AGREE ● TEND TO AGREE ● TEND TO DISAGREE ● STRONGLY DISAGREE ● I DON'T KNOW

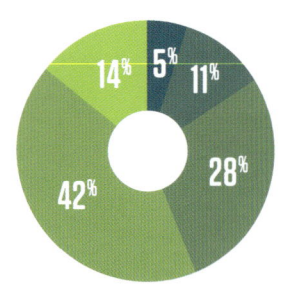

The Bible is totally accurate in all of the principles it teaches
- Strongly agree: 5%
- Tend to agree: 11%
- Tend to disagree: 28%
- Strongly disagree: 42%
- I don't know: 14%

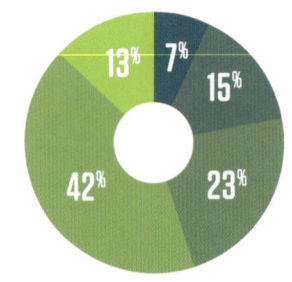

The single, most important purpose of your life is to love God with all your heart, mind, soul and strength
- Strongly agree: 7%
- Tend to agree: 15%
- Tend to disagree: 23%
- Strongly disagree: 42%
- I don't know: 13%

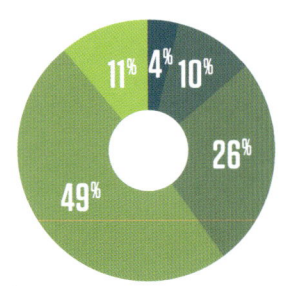

You, personally, have a responsibility to tell other people your religious beliefs
- Strongly agree: 4%
- Tend to agree: 10%
- Tend to disagree: 26%
- Strongly disagree: 49%
- I don't know: 11%

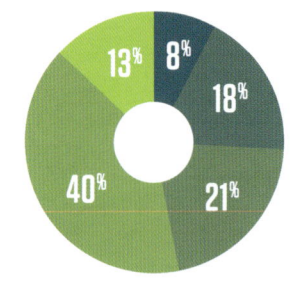

You have made a personal commitment to Jesus Christ that is still important in your life today
- Strongly agree: 8%
- Tend to agree: 18%
- Tend to disagree: 21%
- Strongly disagree: 40%
- I don't know: 13%

Your religious faith is very important in your life today
- Strongly agree: 10%
- Tend to agree: 19%
- Tend to disagree: 24%
- Strongly disagree: 37%
- I don't know: 11%

When you die you will go to Heaven because you have confessed your sins and accepted Jesus as your Saviour
- Strongly agree: 7%
- Tend to agree: 17%
- Tend to disagree: 18%
- Strongly disagree: 38%
- I don't know: 22%

If a person is generally good, or does enough good things for others during their life, they will go to heaven
- Strongly agree: 8%
- Tend to agree: 27%
- Tend to disagree: 12%
- Strongly disagree: 31%
- I don't know: 22%

Everyone goes to heaven when they die, because God loves all people
- Strongly agree: 4%
- Tend to agree: 16%
- Tend to disagree: 21%
- Strongly disagree: 34%
- I don't know: 25%

At the opposite end of the belief spectrum among self-identified Christians are evangelicals. For the purposes of this research, Barna adopted a definition of 'evangelical' based on David Bebbington's four-part rubric, known as the 'Bebbington quadrilateral'. Only those who meet all four of the following standards qualify as 'evangelical' under this definition.

The first principle of Bebbington's rubric is 'biblicism', a perception of the Bible as totally accurate or authoritative in all of its teachings. One in six among all Scots meets this standard (17%). Surprisingly, young adults ages 18 to 24 are more likely than the average to view the Bible in this way (24%).

The next principle is 'crucicentrism', a focus on Christ's atoning work on the cross. Individuals who are crucicentric have confessed their sins and accepted Jesus as their Saviour. About one-quarter of Scottish adults meet this standard (23%).

The third principle is 'activism', or the belief that the gospel must be shared with others. Someone who holds this conviction believes that he has a personal responsibility to share his faith with others. One out of seven Scots meets this standard (14%).

The fourth and final principle of Bebbington's rubric is 'conversionism', a belief that conversion to Christianity is imperative for every person. To meet this standard, self-identified Christians had to 'strongly disagree' that 'everyone goes to Heaven when they die, because God loves all people' or that 'if a person is generally good, or does enough good things for others during their lifetime, they will go to Heaven'. Based on these answers, one in eight adults meets this standard (12%).

Combined, these four principles create the definition for 'evangelical' used in this research. In Scotland today, about three per cent of all adults—five per cent of self-identified Christians—qualify as evangelical. These believers are much less likely than the average to describe Scotland as 'a Christian nation' (8% compared to 31%); rather, they tend to say that 'a secular nation' (40%) or 'a post-Christian nation' (44%) is a more accurate description.

Falling in the middle along the spectrum of Christian belief, between legacy Christians and evangelicals, are self-identified Christians who might be categorised as 'non-evangelical born again' Christians. They do not qualify as evangelical under the Bebbington rubric, yet, in contrast to legacy Christians, they express personal faith in Jesus. Non-evangelical born again Scots report having made a commitment to Christ that is still important in their life today and having confessed their sins and accepted Jesus as Saviour. One-quarter of self-identified Christians fall into this category (26%), about 15 per cent of the total Scottish population.

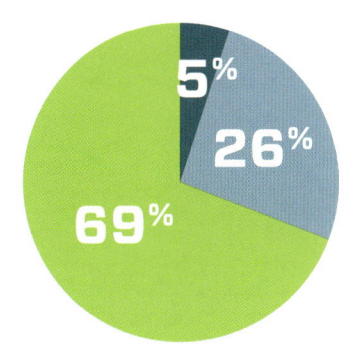

BELIEF SEGMENTS AMONG CHRISTIANS

% AMONG SELF-IDENTIFIED CHRISTIANS

- EVANGELICAL — 5%
- NON-EVANGELICAL BORN AGAIN — 26%
- LEGACY CHRISTIAN — 69%

Even more interesting are the Scots who do not self-identify as 'Christian' but who report having made a personal commitment to Jesus Christ that is still important in their life today and say they have accepted him as their Saviour (2%). In combined percentages that reflect real numbers, this means that more than 800,000 adults in Scotland (17%) have a significant connection to Jesus.

CHRISTIANITY IN SCOTLAND

THE GOOD NEWS

- **61%** of adults have attended church regularly at some point in their life
- **55%** of Scots have an overall favourable impression of Christianity
- **61%** of Scots agree Christianity has good values and principles
- **69%** of adults believe a church is a favourable thing for a community
- **46%** of Scots say it's accurate to describe present-day Christianity in Scotland as consistently showing love for other people

THE BAD NEWS

- **70%** of 18-24 year old adults say the reason they don't attend church is because they just aren't that interested in religion
- **63%** of Scots say they never read the Bible
- **26%** of Scots say Christianity is relevant to their life
- **53%** of adults describe present-day Christianity in Scotland as 'judgmental'
- **61%** of adults disagree that faith is very important in their life today

Christian Practice

In addition to belief, another lens through which we can view the Scottish Christian community is that of religious practices. In the Barna study, 'practising Christian' is a self-identified Christian who attends church at least once a month and says her faith is very important in her life. About one in eight among all Scots (12%)—one in four self-identified Christians (23%)—is in this category. By contrast, a 'non-practising Christian' is a self-identified Christian who either does not attend church at least once a month or says faith is not important, or both. Non-practising Christians represent 40 per cent of the total adult population or 77 per cent of self-identified Christians.

Nearly half of practising Christians say their faith has 'transformed' their lives (47% compared to 16% among all adults) and another 43 per cent say their faith has been 'helpful' but not necessarily transformative (compared to 36% among all adults). Similarly, a majority of practising Christians 'strongly agree' that their faith is relevant to their life (52%). That is more than eight times the number of non-practising Christians who say the same (6%). A majority of non-practising Christians report that faith has not made much of a difference in their life (57%); just 5 per cent say their life has been transformed by faith and one-third say their faith has been helpful but not transformative (33%)—on par with the national average (36%).

PRACTISING & NON-PRACTISING CHRISTIANS

% AMONG ALL ADULTS, BY AGE

● PRACTISING CHRISTIAN   ● NON-PRACTISING CHRISTIAN   ● ALL CHRISTIAN

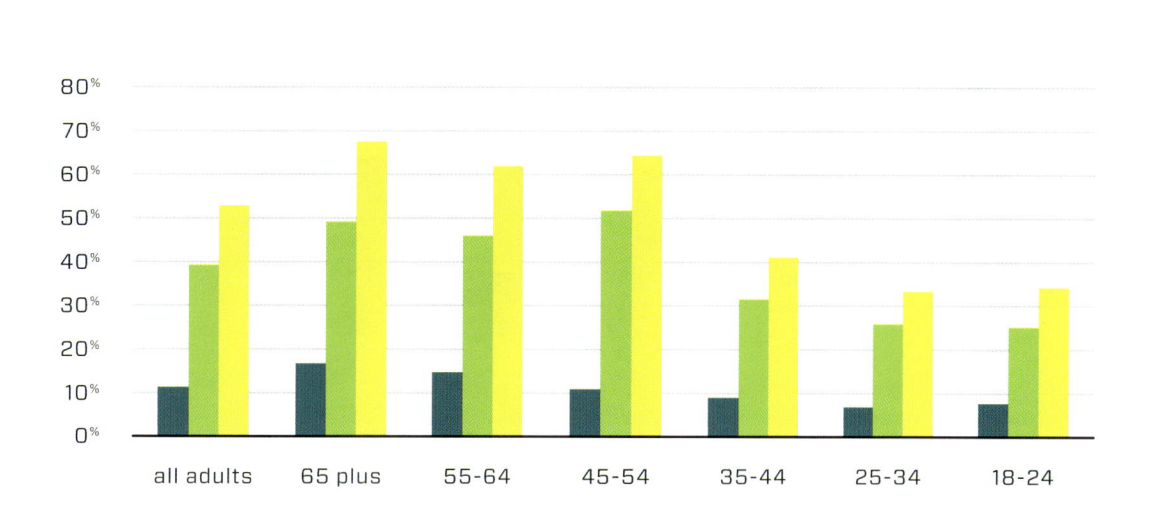

Nine out of 10 non-practising Christians are unchurched (93%), including 86 per cent who are 'dechurched', meaning they attended church at some point in their lives but not in the past six months. Among non-practising Christians who have not attended a church service in the past year, one-third feels that church does not have anything to offer them (32%); 29 per cent say they are simply not interested in religion; and 16 per cent feel they simply don't have time to get involved with church.

One-third of practising Christians report reading the Bible on at least a weekly basis (34%), not including while at church or in group study. On the other hand, nearly six in 10 non-practising Christians say they never read the Bible (56%). When we compare the beliefs of practising and non-practising Christians, there is, as one might suspect, remarkable disparity. To take just one example, beliefs about the Bible, see the following chart for a side-by-side comparison of practising and non-practising Christians' views of Scripture.

BELIEFS ABOUT THE BIBLE AMONG PRACTISING & NON-PRACTISING CHRISTIANS

% AMONG SELF-IDENTIFIED CHRISTIANS

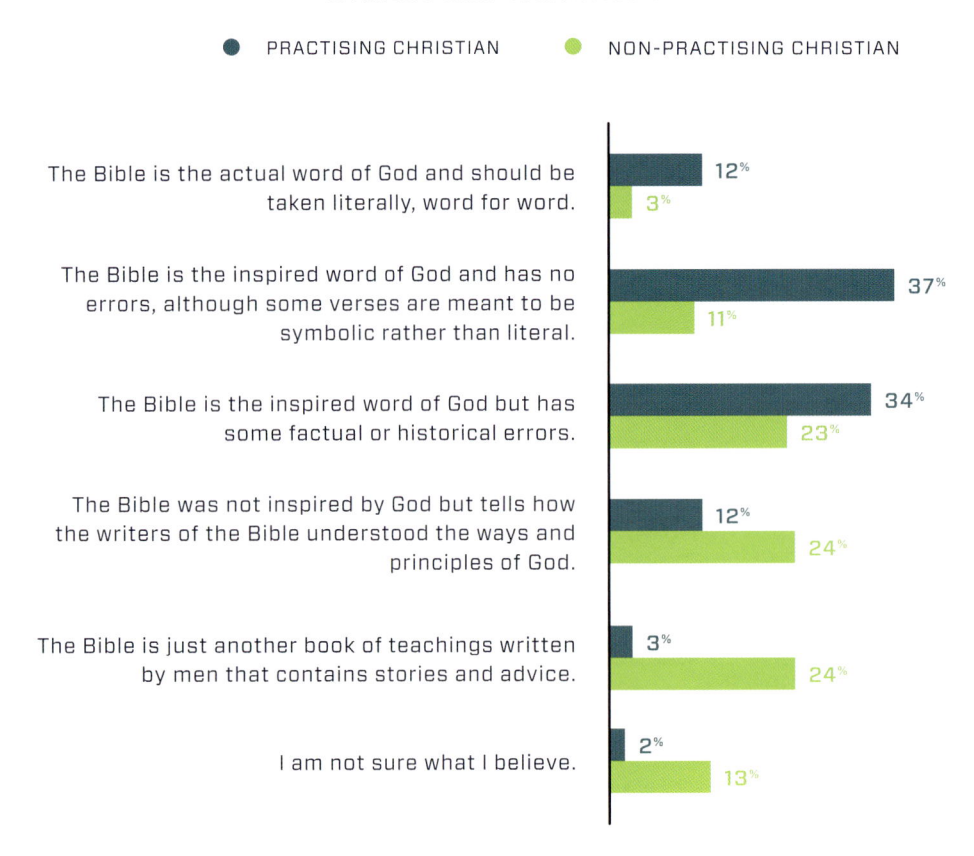

● PRACTISING CHRISTIAN   ● NON-PRACTISING CHRISTIAN

Belief	Practising	Non-Practising
The Bible is the actual word of God and should be taken literally, word for word.	12%	3%
The Bible is the inspired word of God and has no errors, although some verses are meant to be symbolic rather than literal.	37%	11%
The Bible is the inspired word of God but has some factual or historical errors.	34%	23%
The Bible was not inspired by God but tells how the writers of the Bible understood the ways and principles of God.	12%	24%
The Bible is just another book of teachings written by men that contains stories and advice.	3%	24%
I am not sure what I believe.	2%	13%

PERCEPTIONS OF CHRISTIANITY & CHURCHES

According to census data, Scotland has seen a precipitous drop in church involvement during the past few decades. Between 1966 and 2006, membership in the Church of Scotland, which remains the largest denomination, declined from 1.2 million to 504,000. By the end of 2013, membership had dropped to fewer than 400,000. In the 2011 census, those who registered as having 'no religion' (37%) outnumbered, for the first time, those who registered as 'Church of Scotland' (32%).

Overall church involvement in Scotland has fallen, but the more dramatic decrease in Church of Scotland membership skews the numbers. From 2005 to the end of 2015 (predicted by Peter Brierley in 2010) membership will have fallen 35 per cent overall, from about 934,000 to 633,000; when the Kirk is excluded, the drop is 8 per cent, from 382,000 to 349,000.

What has precipitated such declines? One clue may lie in the ways adults describe present-day Christianity in Scotland. Presented with a list of possible descriptors in the Barna research, respondents were asked to rate each on a scale from 'very accurate' to 'not at all accurate'. The phrases most frequently chosen as 'not at all accurate' include 'relevant to my life' (42%), 'not accepting of other faiths' (27%), 'offers hope for the future' (22%) and 'a faith that I respect' (19%). Those most commonly considered 'very accurate' include 'not compatible with science' (23%), 'judgmental' (21%), 'out of touch with reality' (20%) and 'hypocritical' (20%).

DESCRIPTIONS OF CHRISTIANITY

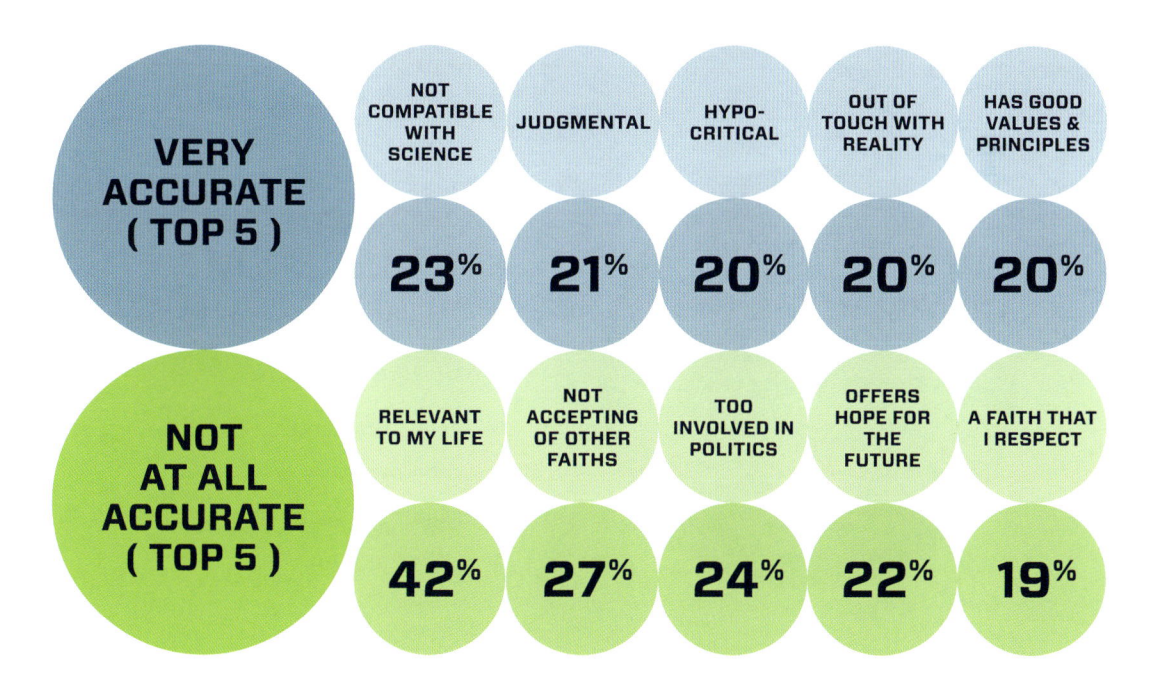

VERY ACCURATE (TOP 5)

Not Compatible With Science	Judgmental	Hypo-critical	Out of Touch with Reality	Has Good Values & Principles
23%	21%	20%	20%	20%

NOT AT ALL ACCURATE (TOP 5)

Relevant to My Life	Not Accepting of Other Faiths	Too Involved in Politics	Offers Hope for the Future	A Faith That I Respect
42%	27%	24%	22%	19%

Given these rather harsh evaluations, one might conclude that the average Scot maintains a negative view of Christianity. Yet a majority reports either a 'very favourable' (12%) or 'fairly favourable' (42%) impression of the faith. Even wider majorities—more than eight in 10—believe a church is a 'very' (24%) or 'fairly' (59%) favourable thing for a community.

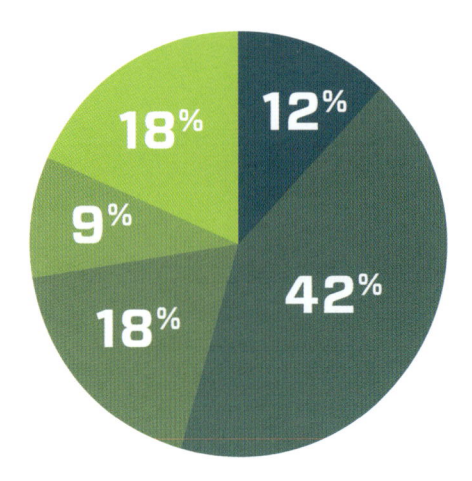

FAVOURABLE / UNFAVOURABLE IMPRESSION OF CHRISTIANITY

% AMONG ALL ADULTS

- VERY FAVOURABLE — 12%
- FAIRLY FAVOURABLE — 42%
- FAIRLY UNFAVOURABLE — 18%
- VERY UNFAVOURABLE — 9%
- DON'T KNOW — 18%

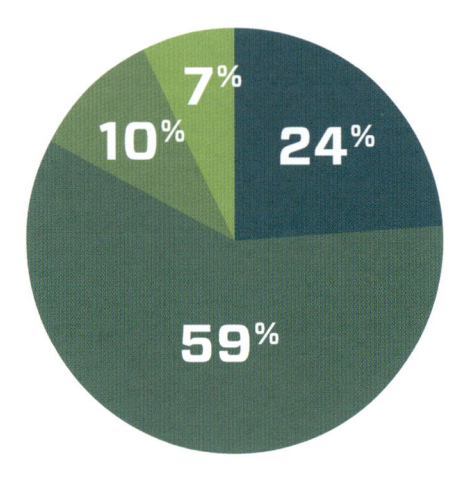

CHURCH IS FAVOURABLE / UNFAVOURABLE FOR A COMMUNITY

% AMONG ALL ADULTS

- VERY FAVOURABLE — 24%
- FAIRLY FAVOURABLE — 59%
- FAIRLY UNFAVOURABLE — 10%
- VERY UNFAVOURABLE — 7%

WHY CHURCH? WHY NOT CHURCH?

A majority of Scots holds favourable views of Christianity and churches, but few make a personal effort to connect with either. What could motivate church attendance? Adults were asked to rate a variety of possible reasons from 'very convincing' to 'not at all convincing'. Seven in 10 find meeting others from the community a 'very' or 'fairly convincing' motivation, and six in 10 consider finding out more about God 'very' or 'fairly convincing'. More than half say religious teaching for their children or improving their own understanding of the Bible might be convincing reasons to attend church.

CONVINCING REASONS TO ATTEND CHURCH

% AMONG ALL ADULTS

● VERY CONVINCING   ● FAIRLY CONVINCING

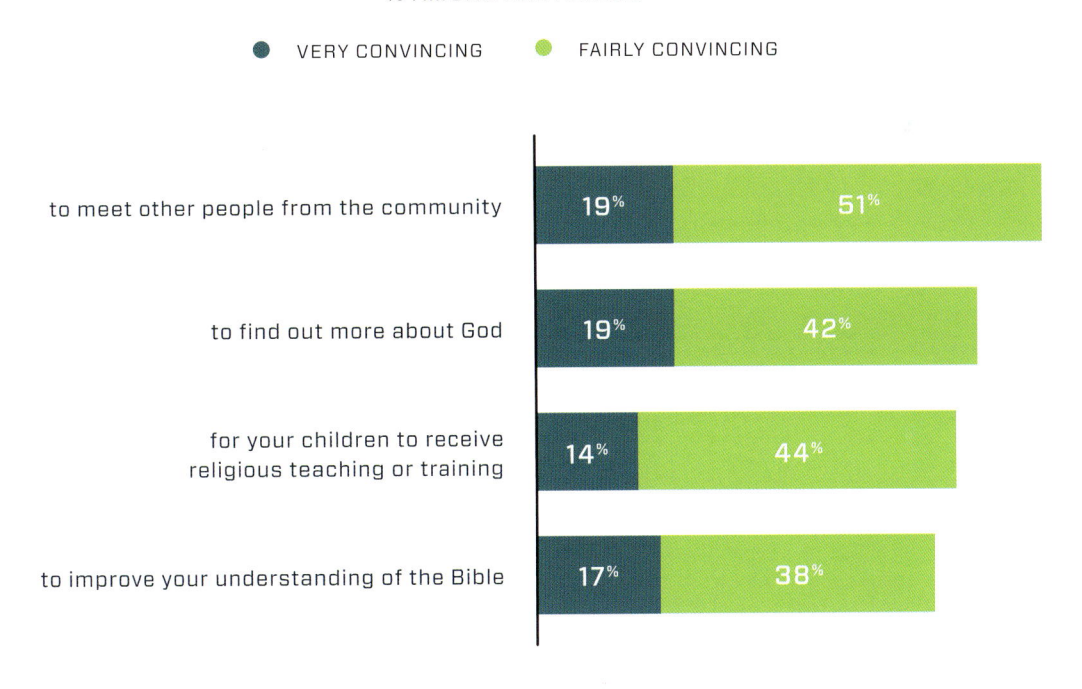

Reason	Very Convincing	Fairly Convincing
to meet other people from the community	19%	51%
to find out more about God	19%	42%
for your children to receive religious teaching or training	14%	44%
to improve your understanding of the Bible	17%	38%

Personal experience with church—or, more accurately, a lack thereof—plays a significant role in young adults' absence from church involvement. Contrasted with the majority of all adult non-attenders whose parents practised Christianity when they were youngsters (52%), just two out of five Scots ages 18 to 24 who do not attend church say their parents practised Christianity (40%). Fewer than half of young-adult non-attenders went to church as children (45%, compared to 61% among all non-attenders), and more than half say they have never in their lives regularly attended church (54%, compared to 30% among all non-attenders).

CHURCH HISTORY

% AMONG ADULTS WHO DO NOT REGULARLY ATTEND CHURCH NOW

● ALL ADULTS   ● ADULTS 18 TO 24

	All Adults	18 to 24	
Growing up, my parents regularly practised Christianity	52%	40%	
I regularly attended church as a child	61%	45%	
I regularly attended church as a teenager	21%	4%	
I have never regularly attended church	30%	54%	

When asked to describe their reasons, eight out of 10 people who do not attend religious services say 'I am just not interested in religion' (50%) or 'the church really does not have anything to offer me' (32%). In that vein, although a majority of Scots views the presence of a Christian fellowship as beneficial (or benign) for a local community, there are substantial differences between the priorities of ministers/pastors and the needs which outsiders believe the church should prioritise.

For example, ministers/pastors of Scottish churches report their top three ministry priorities are preaching and teaching (67%), worship (44%) and discipleship and spiritual growth (42%). Scottish adults, meanwhile, believe that a church's top priorities should be to provide a place where everyone is accepted (50%), to offer activities to keep local teens out of trouble (44%) and to feed the needy (40%). (By a positive turn, a majority of churches in Scotland offers programmes to meet some of these needs: Two-thirds have programmes for youth or teens, and half provide a food bank.)

MINISTRY PRIORITIES & PROGRAMMES VS. COMMUNITY NEEDS

Pastors' top three ministry priorities:
- 67% preaching and teaching
- 44% worship
- 42% discipleship and spiritual growth

What Scottish adults believe should be a church's top priorities:
- 50% providing a place where everyone is accepted
- 44% keeping kids off the streets / activities for teens in the community
- 40% feeding the needy

Top three ministry programmes currently offered by churches in Scotland:
- 65% programmes for youth or teenagers
- 50% a food bank
- 50% mums and toddlers groups

Regardless what combination of ministries is offered by their churches, sizeable majorities of ministers/pastors agree on the factors that are 'extremely important' to transform people's lives for the sake of the gospel. Unfortunately, not many ministers/pastors would rate their church as 'extremely effective' on these factors. Most dramatically, for example, nearly nine out of 10 say that 'bringing people who are not Christian to relationship with Jesus' is extremely important to transform people's lives (86%)—but just two per cent of ministers/pastors would rate their church as extremely effective in this area.

MINISTRY PRIORITIES VS. CHURCH EFFECTIVENESS

PASTORS THINK THE FOLLOWING PRIORITIES ARE EXTREMELY IMPORTANT VS. HOW EFFECTIVE THEY BELIEVE THEIR CHURCH IS AT EXECUTING ON THOSE PRIORITIES

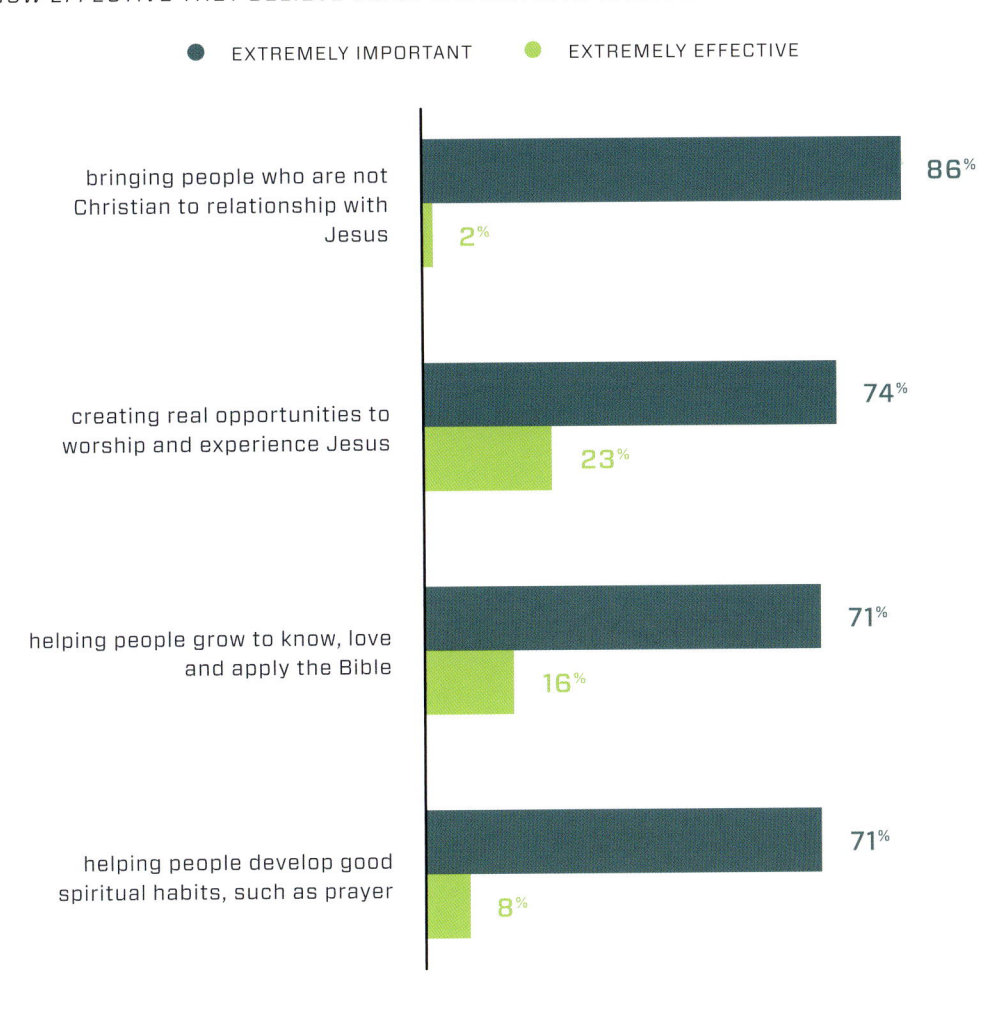

● EXTREMELY IMPORTANT ● EXTREMELY EFFECTIVE

Priority	Extremely Important	Extremely Effective
bringing people who are not Christian to relationship with Jesus	86%	2%
creating real opportunities to worship and experience Jesus	74%	23%
helping people grow to know, love and apply the Bible	71%	16%
helping people develop good spiritual habits, such as prayer	71%	8%

AN EXPERIENCE OF FAITH

Against a receding tide of Christian faith and practice in Scotland advance a fervent few whose lives have been transformed by faith. Scots under the age of 45 are twice as likely (23%) as those 45 and older (12%) to say faith 'has transformed my life'. Younger adults are significantly less likely than older adults, by a margin of nine percentage points, to say faith 'has not made much of a difference' (39% vs. 48%) or that faith 'has been helpful but has not greatly transformed me' (34% vs. 43%). As it is comparatively rare for young Scots to have been raised in church, it may be that a greater proportion of young adults are Christian by choice, rather than by cultural default.

MY PERSONAL FAITH HAS…

% AMONG ADULTS WHO REPORT HAVING A RELIGIOUS FAITH

● ADULTS OVER 45   ● ADULTS UNDER 45

	Adults Over 45	Adults Under 45
… had a negative impact on my life	1%	1%
… not made much of a difference in who I am and how I live	48%	39%
… been helpful but has not greatly transformed me	43%	34%
… transformed my life	12%	23%

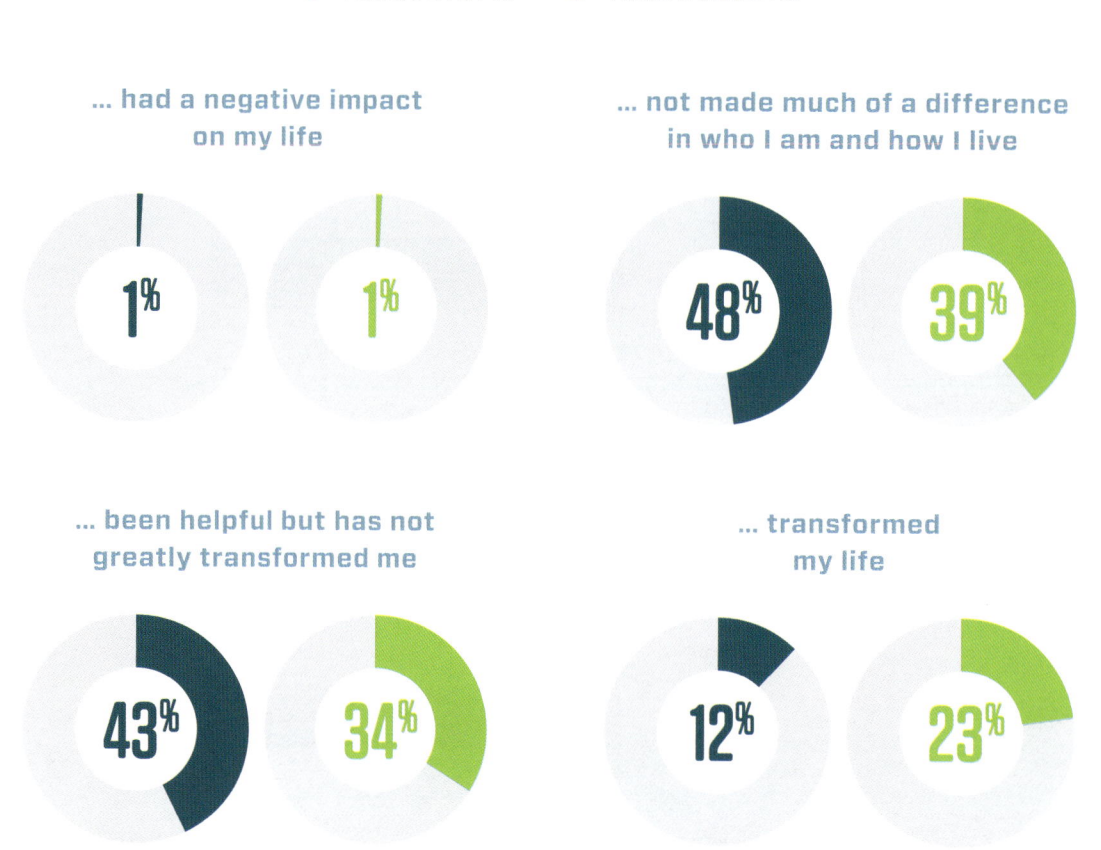

BELIEFS ABOUT THE BIBLE

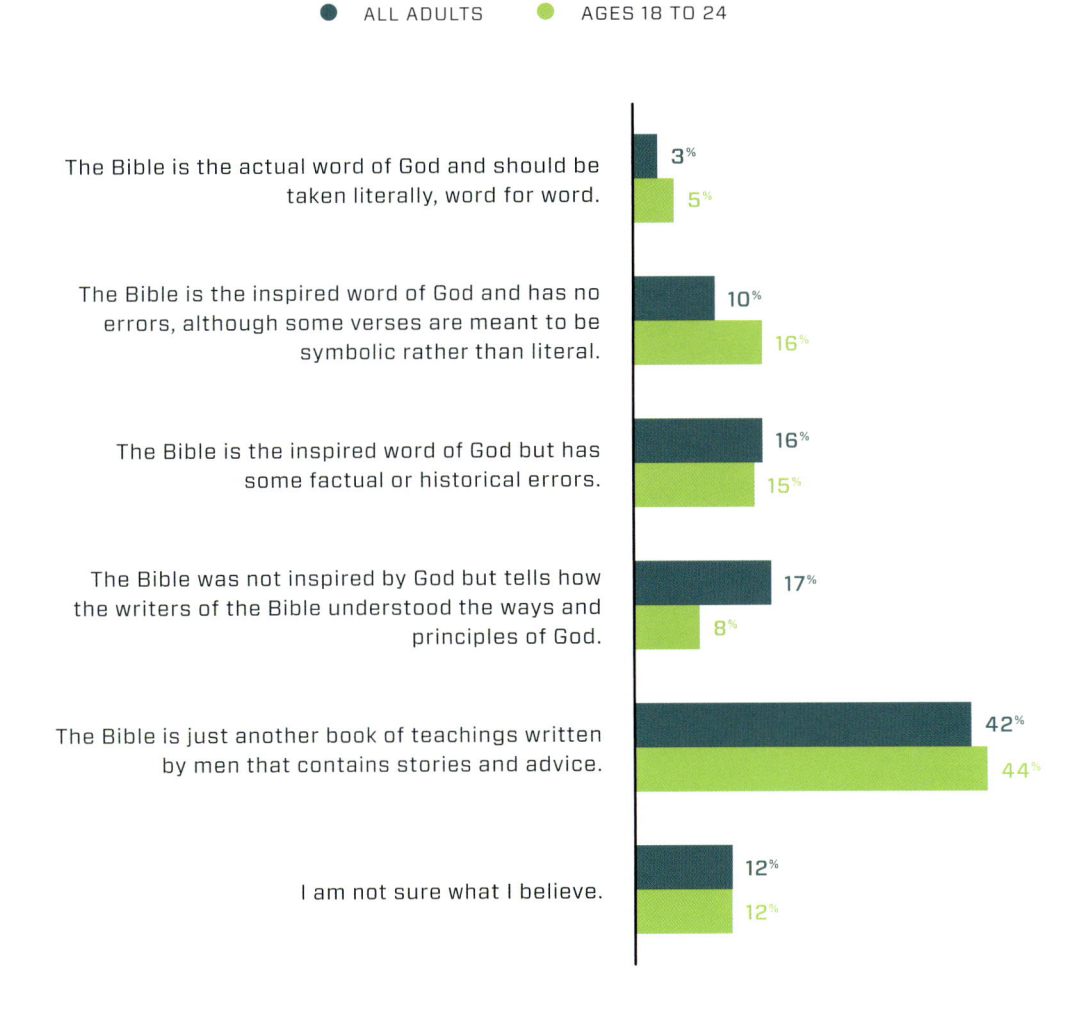

% AMONG ALL ADULTS

● ALL ADULTS ● AGES 18 TO 24

Belief	All Adults	Ages 18 to 24
The Bible is the actual word of God and should be taken literally, word for word.	3%	5%
The Bible is the inspired word of God and has no errors, although some verses are meant to be symbolic rather than literal.	10%	16%
The Bible is the inspired word of God but has some factual or historical errors.	16%	15%
The Bible was not inspired by God but tells how the writers of the Bible understood the ways and principles of God.	17%	8%
The Bible is just another book of teachings written by men that contains stories and advice.	42%	44%
I am not sure what I believe.	12%	12%

Noteworthy, as well, are the 36 per cent of young adults ages 18 to 24 who hold to an orthodox view of the Bible, compared to 29 per cent of all adults (see chart above). They also express more interest in what wisdom the Bible has for their lives (see chart on the following page). By the reverse token, however, young adults are somewhat more likely than the national average (32%) to understand Jesus as 'just a moral teacher or prophet and not God' (37%), and twice as likely as the average (7%) to say that Jesus 'was not an actual historical person' (12%). Such generational cognitive dissonance may be the natural result of few formative church experiences.

INTEREST IN LEARNING FROM THE BIBLE

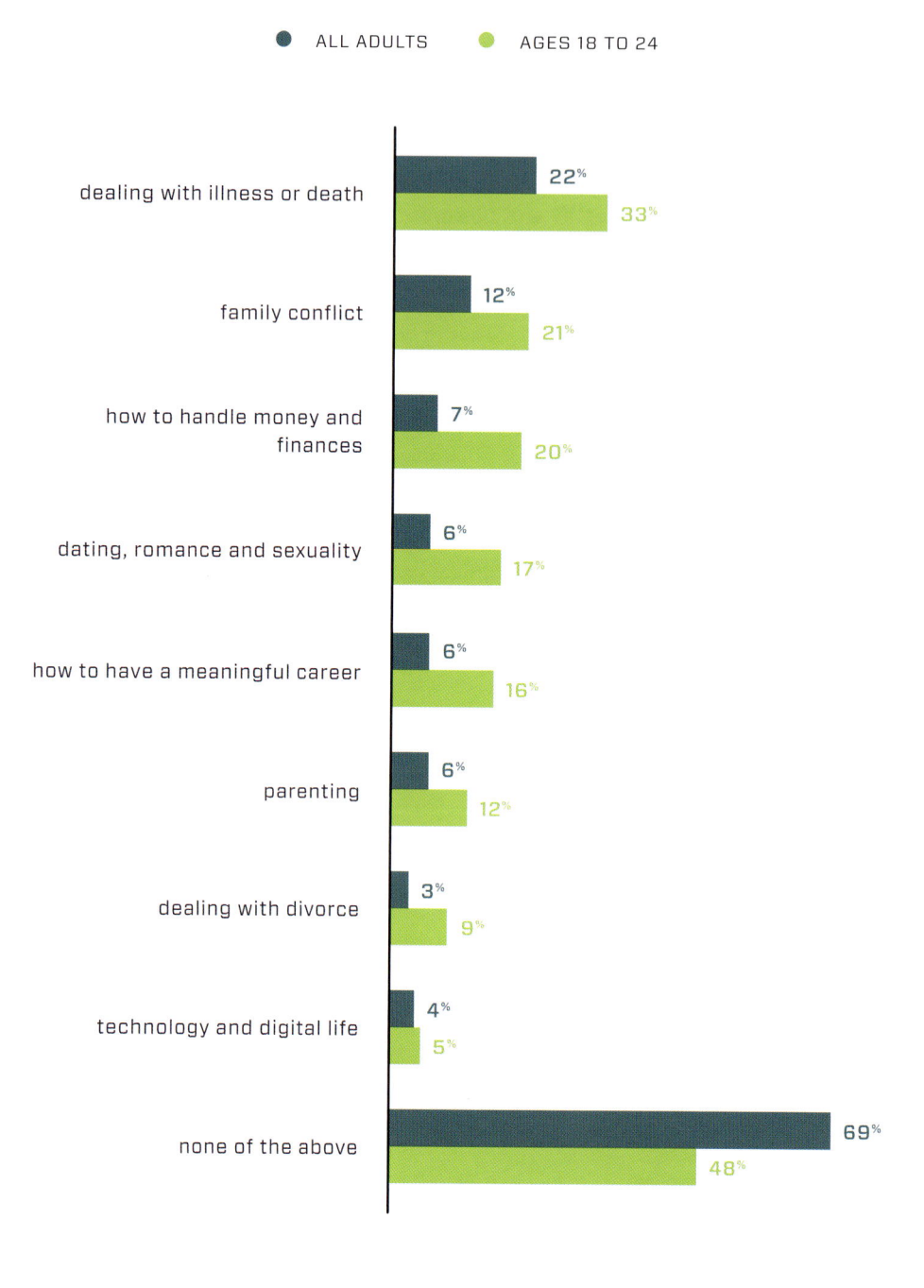

% AMONG ALL ADULTS

- ALL ADULTS
- AGES 18 TO 24

Topic	All Adults	Ages 18 to 24
dealing with illness or death	22%	33%
family conflict	12%	21%
how to handle money and finances	7%	20%
dating, romance and sexuality	6%	17%
how to have a meaningful career	6%	16%
parenting	6%	12%
dealing with divorce	3%	9%
technology and digital life	4%	5%
none of the above	69%	48%

PROFILE OF PASTORS IN SCOTLAND

BY THE NUMBERS

76% — 3 out of 4 pastors say they are optimistic about ministry in Scotland

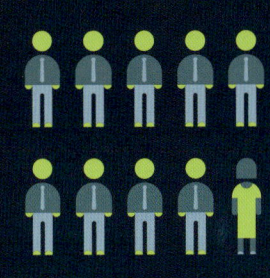

3 out of 4 pastors are 50 or older — **76%**

87% — 9 out of 10 pastors are male

54% of pastors describe Scotland as 'post-Christian'

1 out of 2 pastors say they do not have a personal coach or mentor

2 out of 3 have a network of ministry peers to provide support and accountability

125 Average attendance at a weekly worship service
35 Average teen and children church attendance

PASTORS' TOP 3 MINISTRY PRIORITIES

67% PREACHING & TEACHING

44% WORSHIP

42% DISCIPLESHIP & SPIRITUAL GROWTH

IN THEIR OWN WORDS

Pastors identify the top challenges facing Christianity in Scotland

- Secularisation
- Nationalism
- Christian sectarianism
- Religious legalism
- Liberalisation
- Anti-institutionalism
- Pagan / folk religions
- Divisions in society

CHRISTIAN LEADERS' VIEWS ON SCOTLAND

National Minister/Pastor Survey

The 200 Protestant ministers/pastors who participated in the national quantitative study are split down the middle on whether ministry in Scotland poses unique challenges compared to ministry in other places. Younger ministers/pastors (64%) and those who have been in ministry fewer than 10 years (61%) are likelier than older (46%) and more seasoned ministers/pastors (46%) to say no, Scotland isn't especially challenging. Similarly, they are more likely than older ministers/pastors to say they are optimistic about ministry in Scotland (81% vs. 73%) and less likely to say they are pessimistic (19% vs. 28%). Those who have been in ministry for 20 years or longer have the most negative outlook on ministry, with three in 10 saying they are pessimistic (29%).

OPTIMISTIC / PESSIMISTIC ABOUT MINISTRY IN SCOTLAND

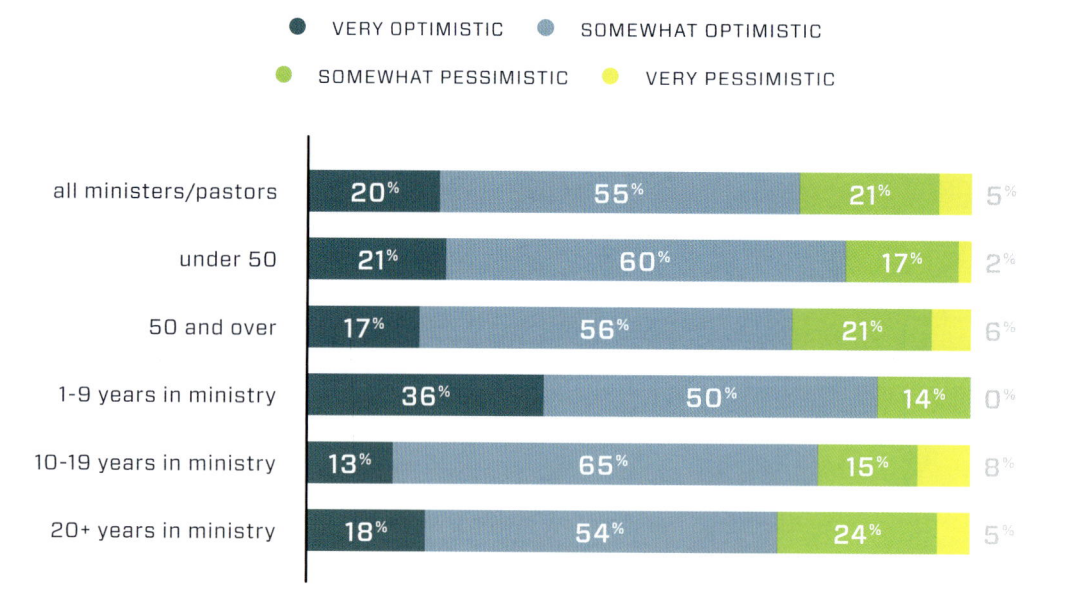

% AMONG ALL MINISTERS/PASTORS

- VERY OPTIMISTIC
- SOMEWHAT OPTIMISTIC
- SOMEWHAT PESSIMISTIC
- VERY PESSIMISTIC

	Very Optimistic	Somewhat Optimistic	Somewhat Pessimistic	Very Pessimistic
all ministers/pastors	20%	55%	21%	5%
under 50	21%	60%	17%	2%
50 and over	17%	56%	21%	6%
1-9 years in ministry	36%	50%	14%	0%
10-19 years in ministry	13%	65%	15%	8%
20+ years in ministry	18%	54%	24%	5%

When we asked ministers/pastors to describe in their own words the specific challenges that are unique to ministry in Scotland, several common themes emerged. These include secularisation, nationalism, Christian sectarianism, religious legalism, liberalisation within the church, a widespread mistrust of institutions, the revival of pagan/folk religions and the fragmentation of society between young and old, urban and rural, rich and poor, northern and southern, and so on.

We also asked those who reported being optimistic about ministry in Scotland to describe the reason or reasons for their positive outlook. By a wide margin, the most common response, phrased in various ways, was 'trust in God'. These leaders see the Holy Spirit at work in fresh ways and believe that, as Scripture promises, nothing will prevail against the church of Jesus Christ.

That said, few ministers would describe Scotland as 'a Christian nation' (5%). Most are under no illusion that Christianity is gaining popularity and cultural cachet among Scots today. 'Post-Christian' was, for a majority, the best descriptor for Scotland (54%), with 'a nation in transition spiritually' preferred by two in five (41%). 'A secular nation' was chosen by one-quarter of all ministers (24%) but was most common among those in ministry for fewer than 10 years (43%).

In-Depth Interviews with Key Christian Influencers

To complement the quantitative survey among 200 ministers/pastors in Scotland, Barna conducted 29 in-depth interviews with Christian leaders of churches, ministries and businesses, handpicked by the Steering Group. Not a single interviewee believes the situation in Scotland is hopeless. Many, however, believe the country will get worse before it gets better, and describe Scotland as 'post-Christian', 'pre-Christian' or simply 'not Christian'.

There are signs of optimism among some leaders who are evolving their ministries in response to the changing culture. Most of these respondents say their ministry is experiencing some level of recent growth, and many of their organisations have common characteristics:

- A priority on the spiritual well-being of their staff and volunteers, encouraging them to attend regular meetings that include Bible study, group book reading, prayer and one-on-one accountability
- A dynamic or charismatic leader in the organisation who has a clear vision and strategy for how to achieve the vision through the ministry's mission
- Clear measures of success and processes for identifying when efforts are not successful; most are clear that they are willing to 'kill' a ministry activity if it does not achieve its objectives
- A focus on spiritual transformation as a primary goal of both the organisation and of the leader(s) personally
- The challenge of raising adequate financial resources
- A lack of qualified leaders—especially younger, potential leaders

What must happen for widespread spiritual transformation to become a reality in Scotland? These leaders report that the most important factor is a move of the Holy Spirit. While there are practical courses of action God's people can take to make space for transformation, leaders agree that, without an act of God, true transformation is not possible.

Not every leader agrees on a way forward, but six main catalysts for change emerged from the interviews.

1. Identify, Train & Empower a New Generation of Leaders

The in-depth interviews revealed that one key driver of transformation will be to raise up leaders from among the younger generations. There is a pervasive sense among the leaders we interviewed that this process has thus far been inadequate, resulting in a profound lack of interest among youth and young adults to lead church movements.

There is also a feeling that leaders of the future will not be of the same type as those in past generations. Some interviewees indicated that future leaders may be on the fringes, may not be obvious and may need support to approach what church looks like in a completely different way. As Graham Duffin of Loanhead Parish Church observed, 'We're still training folk to keep the old going. We need to be training folk for the new'. It is important, as well, for current leaders not to be threatened by developing the next generation, and to discern the most appropriate time to pass the baton. Even so, this will not likely be a quick and easy process.

I think you're talking twenty years to begin to turn the tide, to start seeing church leaders trained to lead missional churches that reach out to people who don't go to church regularly. You'll see that pipeline of people becoming Christians, then becoming leaders, never forgetting how they were before they became Christians, and then leading different types of churches that can reach people like them.
(Dave Richards, Rector of St. Paul's and St. George's Episcopal Church)

Many respondents expressed concerns about effective leader training and argue that educating and equipping tomorrow's leaders will not happen without new strategies. Some say training should be done in collaboration with established educational institutions in Scotland, but there is also a growing trend of 'hub churches' that act as local resource centres to facilitate leadership training. These hub churches are less interested in denomination and more focused on equipping and sending out leaders.

2. Encourage Entrepreneurship in Ministry & Mission

The concept of entrepreneurship and innovation came up many times among those we interviewed. The general feeling is that, because the current situation is so desperate, the church must become more accepting of risk, more open to new strategies and more willing to fail. An entrepreneurial approach to mission is ready to acknowledge when activities or projects are not achieving the hoped-for results, and willing to shut them down in order to try a different approach.

Such a shift toward risk-taking may be difficult, according to Alison Urie, founder of Vox Liminis: 'I don't think the church culture or the way our Scottish society works is very good at taking risks and letting things try and fail. I think there's high pressure, when setting up something new, to make it work. . . . That attitude is one of the biggest challenges that stifles growth, that stifles innovation, that stifles spiritual growth'.

3. Foster Unity among the Whole Body of Christ in Scotland

The Scottish church has a long history of disunity, and most respondents mentioned the presence of divisions within the church as a major impediment to transformation. There is a general consensus that divisions must be healed in order to gain momentum, and leaders share a desire to explore various ways reconciliation might happen.

Church unity refers not only to unity within the Church of Scotland, but also to comity between denominations. A few respondents offered examples of churches from different denominations forming local 'gospel coalitions'. These associations are widely perceived as making a positive impact, not only within the churches but also in their local communities. Remarks from Charity Bowman-Webb of Blue Flame are emblematic of many leaders' sentiments: 'I think we're going to become a lot more connected in Scotland in general—ministries, churches and leaders—because it's dawning on lots of us that we can only accomplish what God is asking us to do with further unity'.

A related theme suggests denominationalism is becoming less important. No one suggested that denominations are now unnecessary, but there is definitely a feeling that historical divisions caused by theological or stylistic differences are no longer a priority. What is a priority is collaborating in order to see spiritual transformation in Scotland.

> *The projects that we've been involved in are gathering believers from a whole range of backgrounds and churches. I think there's something really important about working together. Especially if our vision is to see a community or a region or a nation discipled—we can't do that on our own. We can make individual disciples on our own, but the Great Commission says to make disciples* of *a nation, not* in *a nation.*
> *(Mark Hadfield, Street Pastors Scotland)*

4. Embrace Relational Models of Church

Another theme that emerged from the interviews is the need to move away from the institutional church toward the relational collective of believers that is the Church. Most respondents agree that trusting, one-to-one, culturally relevant relationships must be embraced and encouraged as the Christian family's way forward. This includes equipping people to live for Christ in the workplace and to become evangelists in that setting. Many respondents mentioned the impact small groups have had on their church. These groups, whether in homes, churches, workplaces or pubs facilitate more intensive relationship-building, greater accountability and more community-embedded disciples.

> *There needs to be a move away from the Christendom model of church and church life, to a post-Christendom missional model which recognises that we are missionaries amongst the people, that to cross the road is as much a mission as to cross the world. This shift is beginning to come about, but it's haphazard. I don't think the institutions of the church are quite ready yet to embrace the seismic shift, the huge paradigm shift, that is required.*
> *(Alan McWilliam, Whiteinch Church of Scotland)*

5. Prioritise Discipleship & Spiritual Formation

In addition to a focus on relational models of church, there is a desire to prioritise depth over breadth—or, to put it another way, to prioritise discipleship health. This means measuring the healthiness of people's relationships with God as a metric of ministry success, rather than focusing simply on attendance numbers. Numbers are important and do act as a measure of church health, but robust spiritual formation needs to be the overarching objective.

> *What we try to express as a church is that we are—that we exist to—equip people to live for Christ in every sphere of life, wherever they've been planted. And to that end, we don't try to get people involved with church; we try to get church involved with people—equipping people to live where they are and to carry out God's mission wherever God has planted them.*
> *(Mark Stirling, Cornerstone Community Church, St. Andrews)*

6. Relearn the Gospel in Relevant Language

There is a general consensus that Christians need to relearn and rebuild their trust in the gospel in order to present it confidently to those around them. As Fred Drummond, Director of Evangelical Alliance Scotland, remarked, 'Christians, even if they understand the gospel, find it difficult to articulate, and they're also very defensive. There's a lack of confidence in the gospel'. That is, unless Christians believe in the gospel, they are unlikely to successfully encourage others to accept it as truth.

One respondent described Scotland as 'pre-Christian', implying that the language needed to communicate the gospel must be reengineered in order to communicate effectively to those who have no biblical knowledge.

> *I think we need to give people different language for speaking about the gospel. We need to help people discover a different, everyday language, rather than a spiritualized language—much like Jesus talked about the everyday. Unless he was speaking to church leaders, he spoke about the everyday and used everyday language.*
> *(Ruth Walker, formerly of Mission Scotland)*

WHAT MAKES A CHURCH GROW?

In an effort to identify what's working among churches in Scotland, Barna Group executed a study comparing the practices and perspectives among leaders and congregations in two types of churches: 'growing' and 'baseline'.

BARNA GROUP INTERVIEWED

83 CHURCH LEADERS

+

426 CONGREGANTS

FROM 2 TYPES OF CHURCHES

BASELINE VS. GROWING

Baseline churches experience limited numerical growth and represent the norm among evangelical churches in Scotland, acting as the 'control group' for the comparison study. **Growing churches** report significant levels of growth. Because spiritual transformation is a difficult reality to measure, numerical growth—specifically, conversion growth, rather than transfer growth—is a quantitative proxy measurement that often indicates transformative ministry.

PART II
BEST PRACTICES FOR TRANSFORMATIVE MINISTRY

After completing research in 2014 to assess the State of Faith in Scotland (examined in Part I of this report), the Barna team turned to exploring the best practices that define 'growing churches' in Scotland, compared to a control group of 'baseline churches'. Barna received sample lists of 'baseline' and 'growing' churches from the Steering Group, who formulated these cohorts based on their familiarity with the Scottish church landscape and on widespread perceptions among the evangelical community of churches that demonstrate extraordinary growth. The researchers then interviewed the leaders and congregations of both church cohorts to assess discernible differences between growing and baseline churches. Note that growing churches are not necessarily larger churches; they are simply distinguished by more substantive growth than the norm.

This section, Part II, delves into the practices and perspectives of these growing churches and how they differ from the norm. The study included 83 church leaders and 426 congregants from growing and baseline churches.

A multitude of caveats must accompany this kind of analysis: 1) 'growing churches' do not represent communities of godlier people; 2) results are limited by the questions we asked and cannot reveal anything outside those areas; 3) survey results are correlative and do not imply causal relationships; and 4) the nature of spiritual transformation is extremely difficult to assess, thus, this research is designed to point toward key characteristics for potential transformation.

The rest of Part II explores the following 10 areas of transformation that emerged from the study:

1. Leader Training & Empowerment
2. Leader Effectiveness & Accountability
3. Church Community
4. The Bible
5. Evangelism & Outreach
6. Serving & Social Justice
7. Prayer & Worship
8. Theology & Religious Activity
9. Stewardship & Vocation
10. Resources & Partnerships

1. LEADER TRAINING & EMPOWERMENT

As the in-depth interviews with Scottish leaders revealed, leadership development is an essential, and urgent, driver of transformation in Scotland. But even before they can be trained, leaders must be identified and then invited into the fraternity of leaders. Too often, established leaders are reluctant to make a personal investment in the next generation.

When asked about what they perceive as the barriers to more effective church leaders in Scotland, ministers/pastors in the national survey offered a variety of responses. Among the themes that emerged from their answers were too many requirements unrelated to calling and giftedness (that is, too many 'official' hoops to jump through); the inflexibility of church structures and bureaucracy; liberalisation among the next generation; inadequate financial, emotional and spiritual support for leaders; and inaccessible, impractical or nonexistent training.

It appears that surmounting these barriers is one key to transformational ministry. Our research shows that growing churches are committed to leadership development. About one-third of leaders (30%) and people in the congregation (36%) say it is 'completely true' that leadership development is a top priority for their faith community, compared to one in 20 baseline leaders (5%) and one in 11 baseline churchgoers (9%). When one combines 'completely' and 'mostly true', the difference is even more plain: Three-quarters of growing church leaders (74%), versus three in 10 baseline leaders (32%), say that leadership development is a top priority.

LEADERSHIP DEVELOPMENT IS A TOP PRIORITY

% AMONG GROWING AND BASELINE CHURCH LEADERS AND CONGREGATIONS

● COMPLETELY TRUE   ● MOSTLY TRUE

	Completely True	Mostly True
baseline church leaders	5%	27%
baseline congregations	9%	32%
growing church leaders	30%	44%
growing congregations	36%	31%

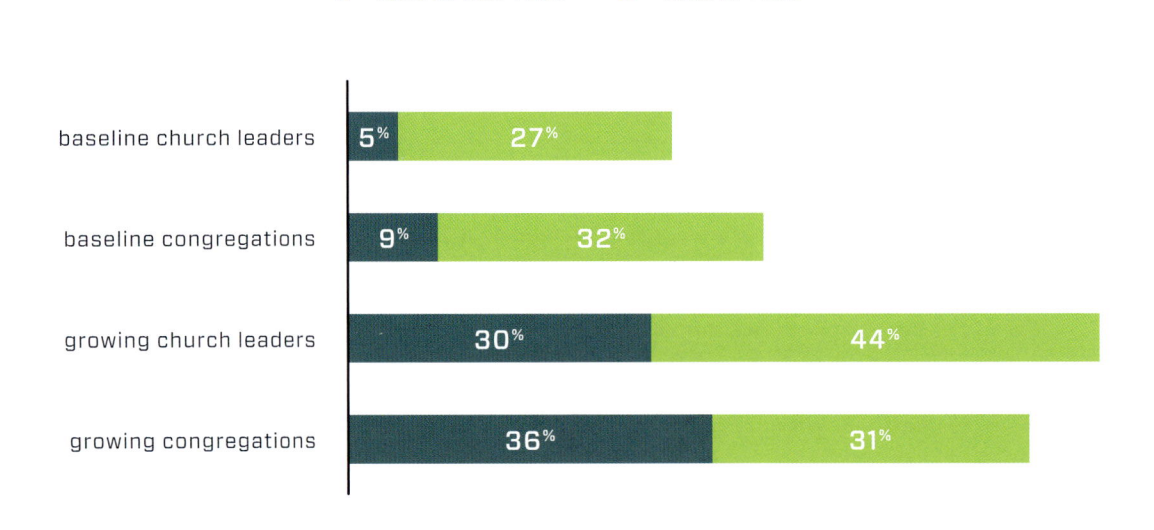

A premium on leader integrity is also significant. Leaders in growing churches tend to have high standards and expectations for themselves and their fellow leaders. Fifty-seven per cent—compared to 13 per cent of baseline leaders—say it is 'completely true' that 'people who are invited to lead in the church must display a godly character, a calling to leadership and be committed to improving as leaders'.

Noteworthy, as well, is the apparent resolve to deepen the bench of willing, capable and empowered leaders. More than twice as many growing (36%) as baseline people in the congregation (16%) say it is 'completely true' that members are encouraged to take on leadership roles in the church. And while one-third of each group reports having received some kind of leadership training from their church, nearly half of growing church congregations rate their training as 'excellent' (46%), compared to just one in five baseline churchgoers who report an excellent training experience (19%).

CONGREGATIONAL LEADERSHIP

% 'COMPLETELY TRUE' AMONG GROWING AND BASELINE CONGREGATIONS

● BASELINE CONGREGATIONS   ● GROWING CONGREGATIONS

Church members are encouraged to take on leadership roles in the church.
- Baseline: 16%
- Growing: 36%

I have personally received leadership training from my church.
- Baseline: 34%
- Growing: 39%

I would rate the quality of the leadership training I received as 'excellent'.
- Baseline: 19%
- Growing: 46%

If theological education is any indication of an ability to train others, it appears that growing church leaders may be somewhat more prepared and equipped to coach young and potential leaders. One-third of growing church leaders (33%) have graduated from some sort of formal theological training, compared to one in five baseline leaders (22%).

2. LEADER EFFECTIVENESS & ACCOUNTABILITY

Closely related to identifying, training and empowering new leaders is adopting a leadership model that relies on a capable team for accountability, shared vision and continuous improvement. Six in 10 growing church leaders feel their leadership team is highly effective (61%), compared to one-quarter of baseline leaders (26%).

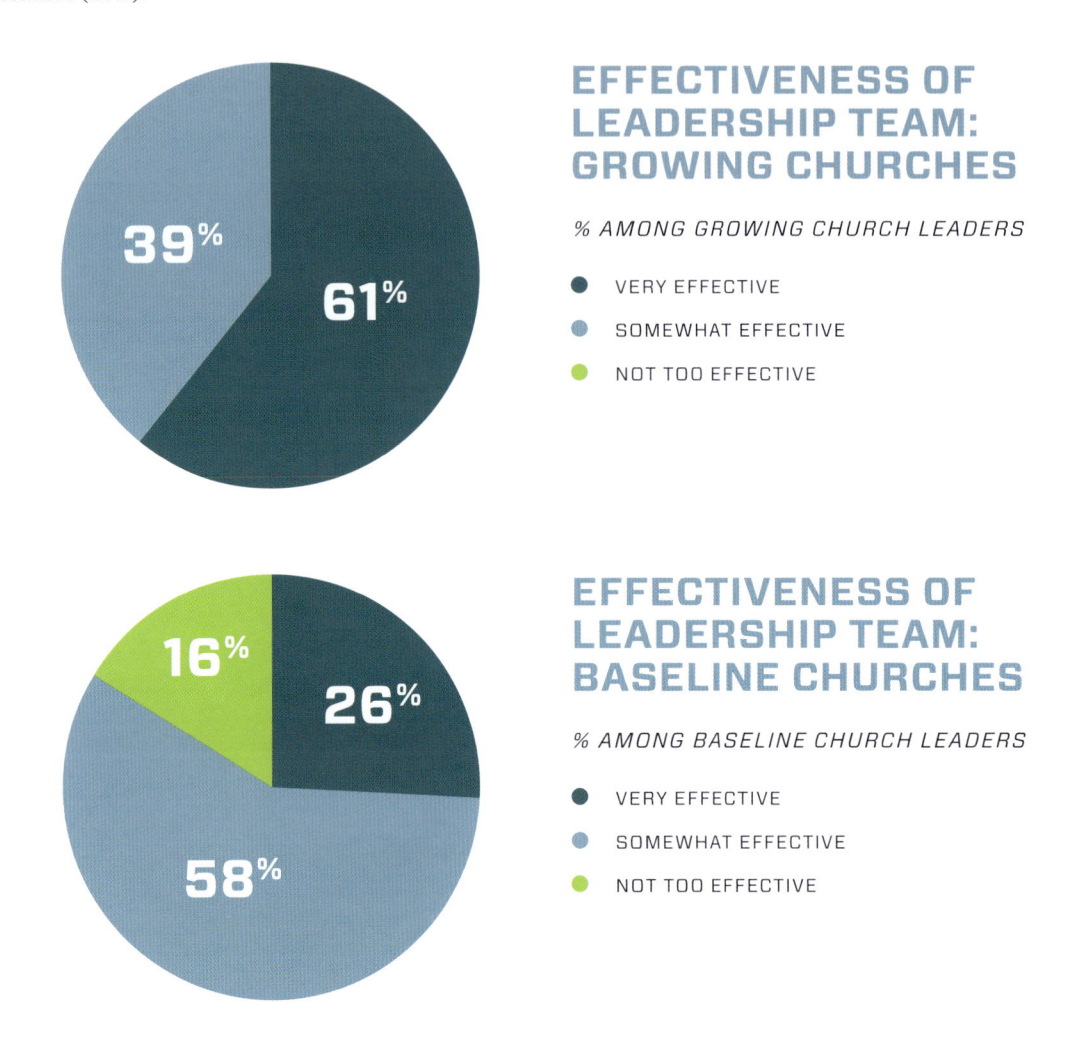

EFFECTIVENESS OF LEADERSHIP TEAM: GROWING CHURCHES

% AMONG GROWING CHURCH LEADERS

- VERY EFFECTIVE: 61%
- SOMEWHAT EFFECTIVE: 39%
- NOT TOO EFFECTIVE

EFFECTIVENESS OF LEADERSHIP TEAM: BASELINE CHURCHES

% AMONG BASELINE CHURCH LEADERS

- VERY EFFECTIVE: 26%
- SOMEWHAT EFFECTIVE: 58%
- NOT TOO EFFECTIVE: 16%

While it is not possible to pinpoint each and every factor that contributes to effectiveness, leaders' answers to specific questions about skills, accountability and development highlight some checks and balances necessary to keep a team on track:

HABITS OF EFFECTIVE LEADER TEAMS

% 'COMPLETELY TRUE' AMONG GROWING AND BASELINE CHURCH LEADERS

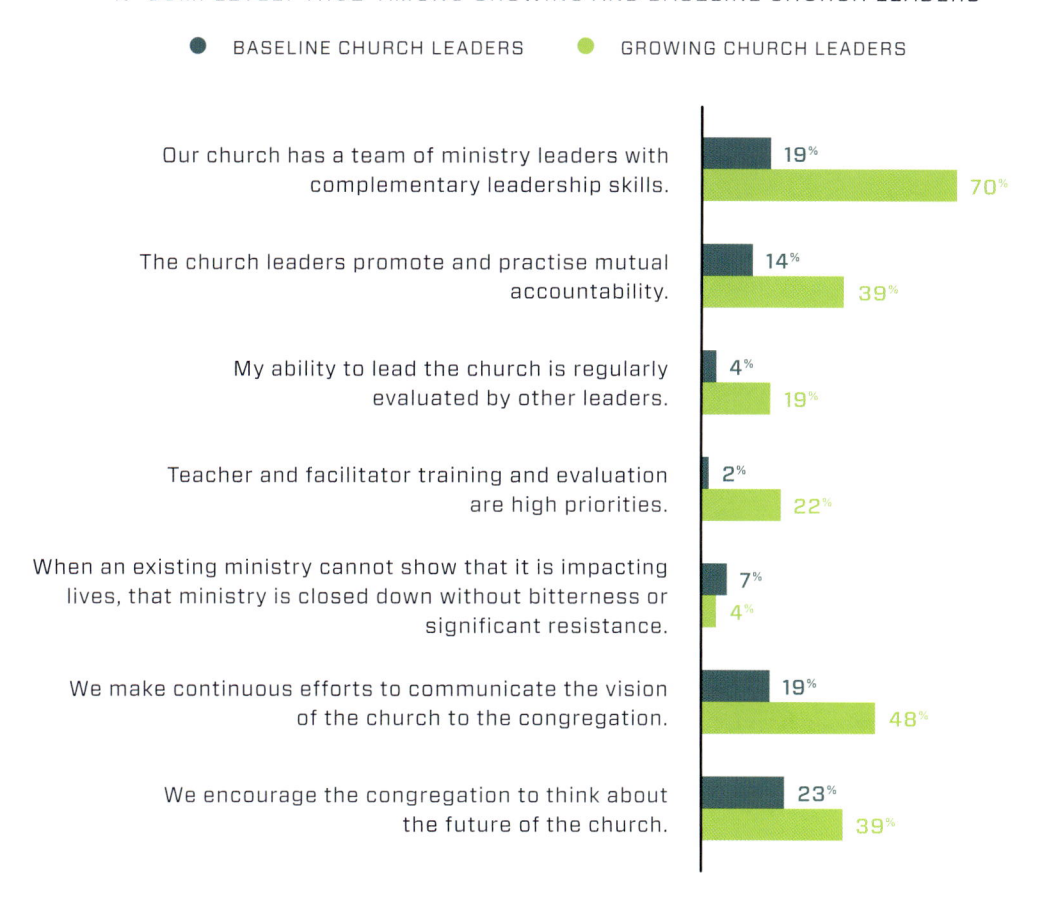

- BASELINE CHURCH LEADERS
- GROWING CHURCH LEADERS

Statement	Baseline	Growing
Our church has a team of ministry leaders with complementary leadership skills.	19%	70%
The church leaders promote and practise mutual accountability.	14%	39%
My ability to lead the church is regularly evaluated by other leaders.	4%	19%
Teacher and facilitator training and evaluation are high priorities.	2%	22%
When an existing ministry cannot show that it is impacting lives, that ministry is closed down without bitterness or significant resistance.	7%	4%
We make continuous efforts to communicate the vision of the church to the congregation.	19%	48%
We encourage the congregation to think about the future of the church.	23%	39%

Seven out of 10 growing church leaders say it is 'completely true' that 'our our church has a team of ministry leaders with complementary leadership skills' (70%), while just one in five baseline leaders says this statement is 'completely true' of their team (19%)—a substantial gap between the two groups. Three-quarters of growing church leaders say their leadership team promotes and practises mutual accountability (74% completely + mostly true), but only 44 per cent of baseline leaders say the same. About half of growing church leaders say their own leadership is regularly evaluated by other team members (48%); only 17 per cent of baseline leaders say they undergo regular team evaluation. Nearly six out of 10 growing church leaders (57%), but fewer than one in seven baseline leaders (13%) say it is 'completely' or 'mostly true' that 'teacher and facilitator training and evaluation are high priorities at the church'. Finally, growing church leaders report a practice of regularly evaluating the transformative effect of various ministries and pruning accordingly (70%); baseline leaders are less likely to ground their ministry evaluations on life transformation (42%).

Beyond empowering a leadership team to be effective, empowering the broader congregation may be transformational. Half of growing church leaders say they regularly communicate the vision of the church to the congregation (48%), while just 19 per cent of baseline leaders say so. Similarly, nearly eight in 10 growing church leaders say it is 'completely' or 'mostly' true that they encourage the congregation to think about the church's future (78%), but just over half of baseline leaders make this a priority (53%). While congregational factors may appear, at first glance, to be tangentially related, a front-and-centre vision likely lends focus and inspiration to the leadership team's efforts.

3. CHURCH COMMUNITY

Belonging is difficult to quantify, but engendering a strong sense of belonging seems to be another hallmark of transformational ministries. The data indicate that, overall, people in growing churches have a stronger, more durable, sense of belonging to their faith community than do baseline churchgoers. On every measure included in the survey, growing churches are rated higher than baseline churches are rated by their membership. Growing church congregations report stronger feelings of belonging and encouragement, and greater confidence that non-Christians would likewise feel welcomed into the community.

A SENSE OF BELONGING

% 'COMPLETELY TRUE' AMONG GROWING AND BASELINE CONGREGATIONS

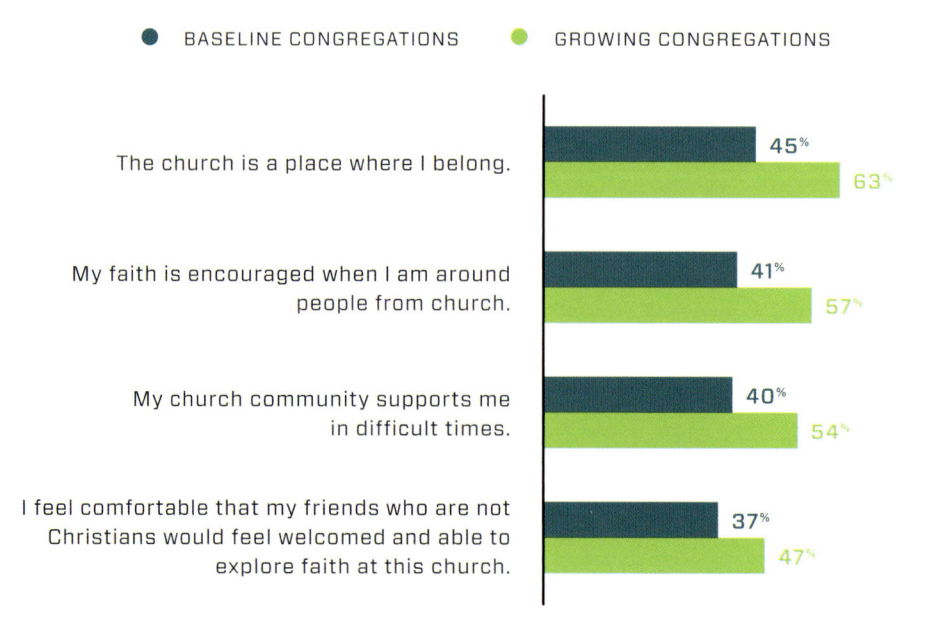

● BASELINE CONGREGATIONS   ● GROWING CONGREGATIONS

Statement	Baseline	Growing
The church is a place where I belong.	45%	63%
My faith is encouraged when I am around people from church.	41%	57%
My church community supports me in difficult times.	40%	54%
I feel comfortable that my friends who are not Christians would feel welcomed and able to explore faith at this church.	37%	47%

Taken together with leader responses, it is clear that these outcomes are deliberately cultivated. Growing church leaders (52%) are much more likely than baseline leaders (19%) to say it is 'completely true' that 'building honest and deep relationships with one another is one of the core values of the church'. It also appears that leaders of growing churches are keen to create a 'safe space' for faith, doubt and questions—but with mixed outcomes. Eight out of 10 say their congregation already is such a community (83%, compared to 39% of baseline leaders), but just half of the people in their congregation 'completely' agree with a similar statement about non-Christian friends feeling welcome and free to explore faith questions (47%). Thus, growing church leaders' answers likely point to something of an aspirational view, rather than a fully formed, current reality.

For almost all the demographic ministry segments, growing churches—both leaders and congregations—report more 'active and healthy' ministries than do baseline churches. Some interesting patterns emerge in this arena:

- Children's ministry receives the highest 'healthy and active' marks across the board, though still higher among growing church leaders (82%) and congregations (74%) than among baseline leaders (54%) and congregations (68%).

- The widest disparity between growing and baseline churches is found in family ministry. While about half of growing church leaders (55%) and congregations (51%) say it's 'completely true' that their family ministry is active and healthy, just one in five baseline leaders (19%) and one-third of baseline congregations (37%) say so about their churches. That is, leaders in baseline churches are notably dissatisfied with their ministry to families.

- Churchgoers in growing churches rate their youth and young adult ministries more highly than do their leaders, which may indicate that those ministries are having a greater impact than leaders believe (if members are reporting based on how those ministries have met their own needs). Growing churches are not much different, statistically speaking, from baseline churches in their ratings of young adult ministry. Furthermore, growing leaders are least satisfied with their ministry to young adults, which is a notable gap given some of the previous findings about the opportunity and need to minister effectively to Scottish young adults.

- Ministry efforts to adults 60+ are rated among the least 'active and healthy'. All respondents feel this is their least effective demographic ministry area out of the five we assessed—except for growing leaders, who rank their young adult ministry as less effective.

ACTIVE & HEALTHY DEMOGRAPHIC MINISTRIES

% 'COMPLETELY TRUE' AMONG GROWING AND BASELINE LEADERS AND CONGREGATIONS

- BASELINE CHURCH LEADERS
- BASELINE CONGREGATIONS
- GROWING CHURCH LEADERS
- GROWING CONGREGATIONS

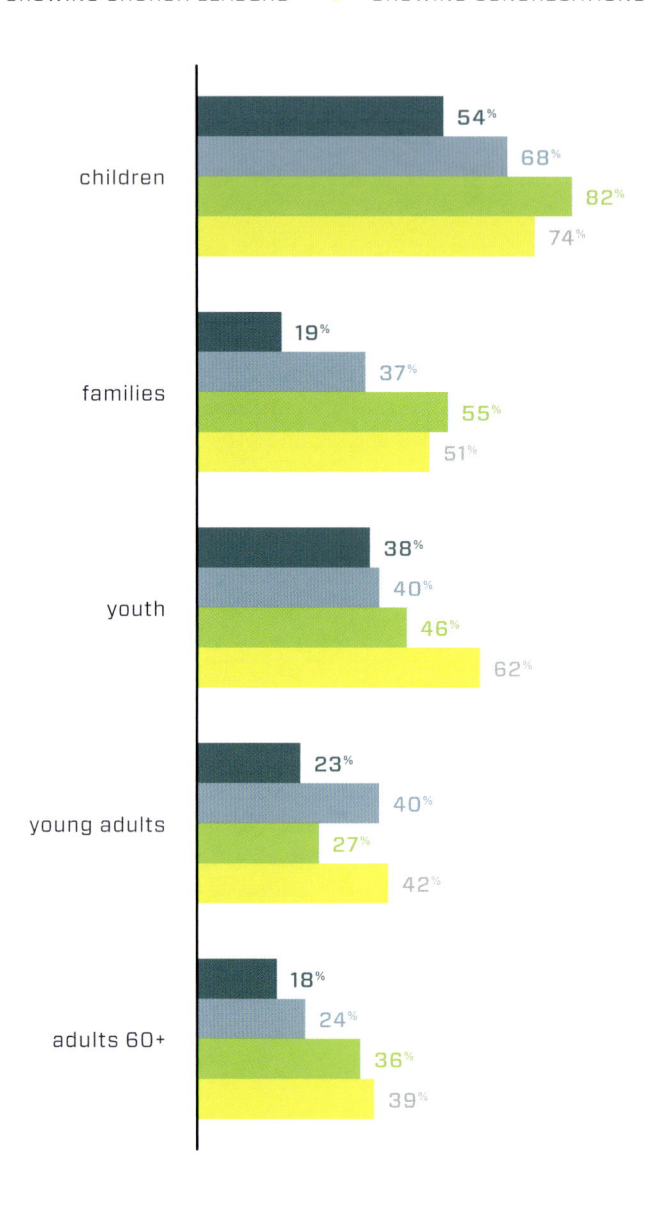

Demographic	Baseline Church Leaders	Baseline Congregations	Growing Church Leaders	Growing Congregations
children	54%	68%	82%	74%
families	19%	37%	55%	51%
youth	38%	40%	46%	62%
young adults	23%	40%	27%	42%
adults 60+	18%	24%	36%	39%

4. THE BIBLE

Bible teaching, Bible study and relevant, Bible-rich expository preaching are all hallmarks of growing churches. Barna identified a major gap in preaching and teaching approaches between growing and baseline churches. Eight in 10 leaders of growing churches say it is 'completely true' that their approach to teaching the Bible is expository (83%), compared to fewer than one in 10 baseline leaders (8%). This is an enormous disparity, and likely indicates an underlying difference in teaching the Bible as a driver of church growth and vitality.

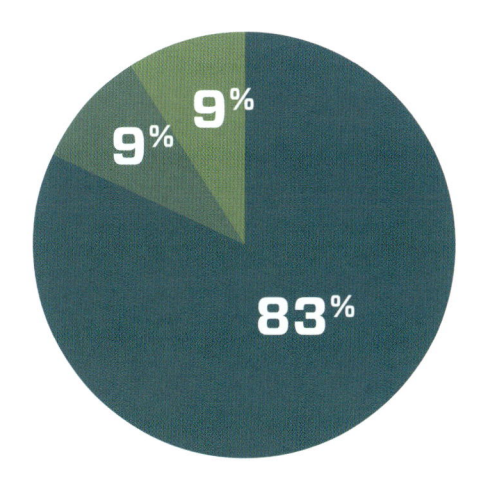

EXPOSITORY APPROACH TO TEACHING THE BIBLE: GROWING CHURCHES

% AMONG GROWING CHURCH LEADERS

- COMPLETELY — 83%
- MOSTLY — 9%
- SOMEWHAT — 9%
- NOT MUCH
- NOT AT ALL

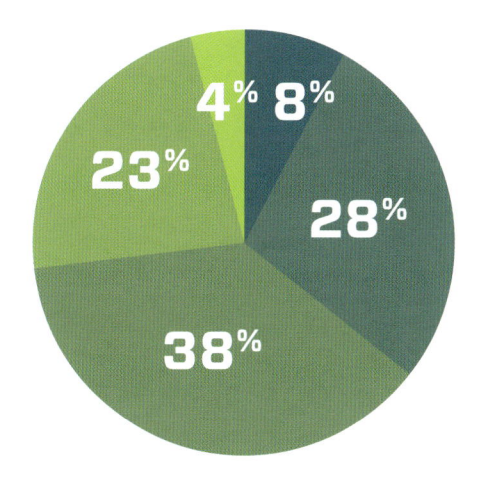

EXPOSITORY APPROACH TO TEACHING THE BIBLE: BASELINE CHURCHES

% AMONG BASELINE CHURCH LEADERS

- COMPLETELY — 8%
- MOSTLY — 28%
- SOMEWHAT — 38%
- NOT MUCH — 23%
- NOT AT ALL — 4%

Along with a systematic approach to Bible teaching, growing church leaders (39%) are also more apt than baseline leaders (17%) to use stories and testimonies to make biblical teaching more relevant to the congregation's lives. They also more consistently marry biblical principles to life application, according to both leaders (83%, compared to 57% baseline) and the people in their congregation (62%, compared to 34% baseline). These teaching strategies seem to bear fruit: More than half of people in growing churches (55%) say it is 'completely true' that 'the Bible teaching I receive in my church is relevant to my life'; only one-quarter of baseline churchgoers say so (27%).

Teaching that is relevant and rich in biblical content appears to foster positive outcomes in people's lives. Those in growing churches (59%) are more ready than baseline members (36%) to report that 'attending church has helped me understand the Bible better'. Twice as many growing church leaders (70%) as baseline leaders (33%) say 'discipleship, Bible teaching and worship at our church help attenders to develop a biblical worldview'. Compared to their leaders, a similar proportion of baseline churchgoers (36%), but somewhat fewer people in growing churches (55%), confirm their leaders' claims.

In what areas of their lives do congregations feel the greatest impact of their church's Bible teaching? Growing and baseline churchgoers report many similarities and a few significant differences. Most notably, two-thirds of people in growing churches say their church's Bible teaching and engagement has helped them grow closer to God (62%), compared with fewer than half of baseline churchgoers (45%). They are also somewhat more likely to say the Bible teaching has helped them be more confident about sharing their faith (34%, compared to 26% baseline). Baseline congregations (14%), on the other hand, are more likely than growing church congregations (6%) to choose 'none of these' from the available options.

MOST SIGNIFICANT IMPACT OF CHURCH'S BIBLE TEACHING

% 'COMPLETELY TRUE' AMONG GROWING AND BASELINE CONGREGATIONS

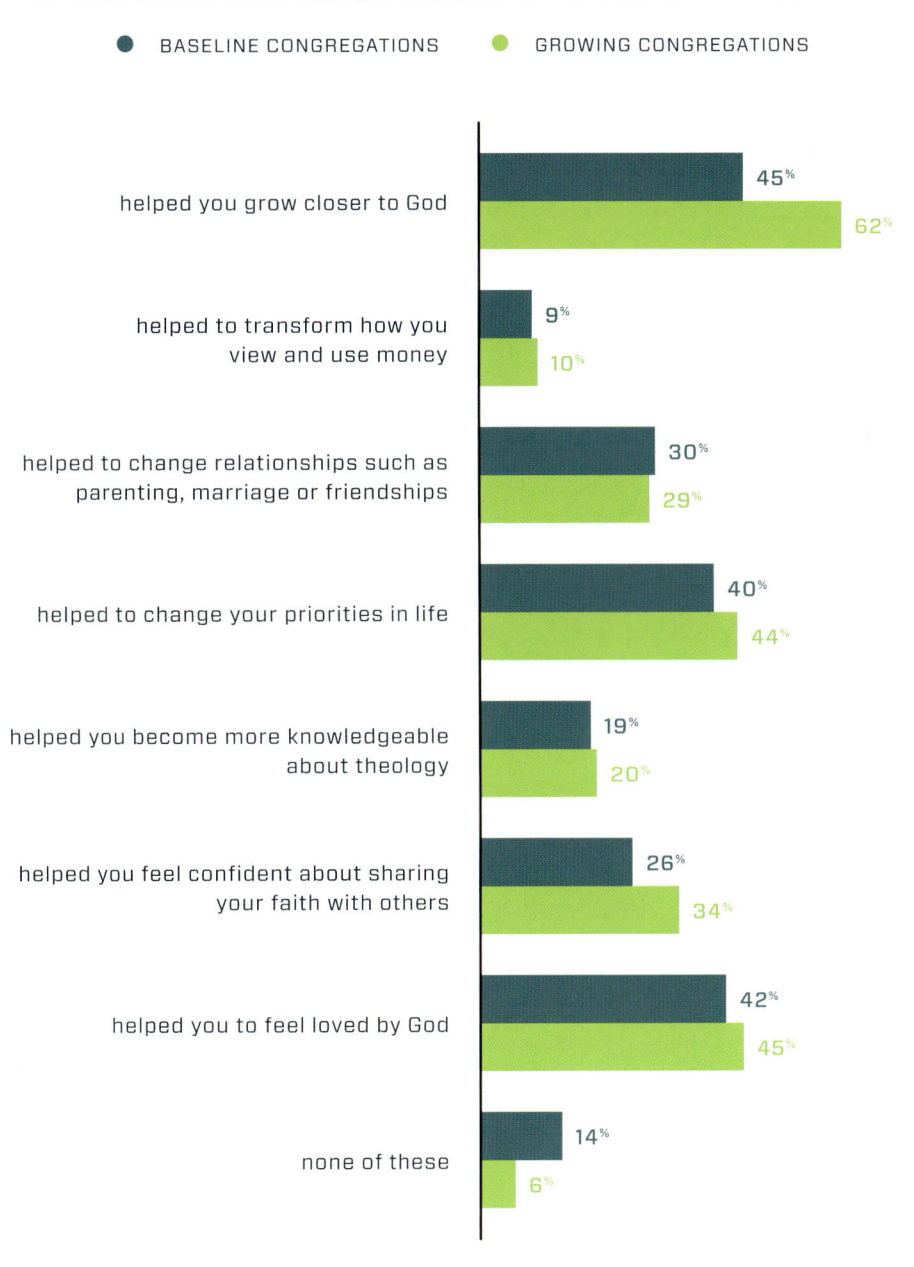

- BASELINE CONGREGATIONS
- GROWING CONGREGATIONS

Impact	Baseline	Growing
helped you grow closer to God	45%	62%
helped to transform how you view and use money	9%	10%
helped to change relationships such as parenting, marriage or friendships	30%	29%
helped to change your priorities in life	40%	44%
helped you become more knowledgeable about theology	19%	20%
helped you feel confident about sharing your faith with others	26%	34%
helped you to feel loved by God	42%	45%
none of these	14%	6%

5. EVANGELISM & OUTREACH

As one might expect, active evangelism is a distinguishing feature of churches whose growth comes primarily through new Christian commitments (conversion growth) rather than from churchgoers switching from one faith community to another (transfer growth). But what specific practices result from a commitment to active evangelism?

Growing church leaders (78%) are twice as likely as baseline leaders (37%) to say their congregation is encouraged to talk with others about their faith in Jesus. Two-thirds of growing (63%) and nearly half of baseline congregations (47%) also say they are encouraged to talk about their faith. (Oddly, a larger proportion of baseline congregations than leaders say encouragement to evangelise is a regular feature of their church experience. It may be that churchgoers have a broader definition of being 'encouraged to talk about faith' than their leaders.) Regardless of an emphasis on personal evangelism, however, few churches of either type have proactive evangelism training programmes: Approximately one in five growing churches and fewer than one in 10 baseline churches report such a programme.

A large majority of growing church leaders (87%) and six in 10 of the people in their congregation (61%) say it is 'completely true' that 'the church teaches that evangelism is more than an event'; nevertheless, about half report their church sponsoring local outreach events (44% leaders; 56% members), which may include evangelism as well as community service. By contrast, one-third of baseline congregations (34%) and one in five leaders (21%) recall such a sponsored event.

On the whole, there is room for improvement among both baseline and growing churches when it comes to welcoming non-Christians. Growing church leaders may be overconfident in their assessment of their church's hospitality: 65 per cent believe non-Christians feel welcome, while only 38 per cent of the people in their congregation share their confidence. Baseline responses indicate an even less approachable environment, with just one in five leaders (19%) and 28 per cent of members saying their church is welcoming to non-Christians. A previous question from the Church Community module reveals that most growing (83% leaders; 58% congregation) and somewhat fewer baseline churches (39% leaders; 36% congregation) consider their church to be a safe place to explore faith and doubt, and to ask questions. Yet non-Christians will not have the opportunity to explore in this way if they are not warmly invited through the doors.

Once new believers become part of the community, growing churches make an intentional effort to coach them along their spiritual journey. Half of growing church leaders say it is 'completely true' of their church that 'evangelism and discipleship are integrated, not isolated; those who accept Christ are consistently nurtured toward maturity' (48%). Just one in 10 baseline leaders reports a similarly intentional transition (9%). This is one of the most significant gaps between baseline and growing leaders.

Given churchgoers' somewhat lukewarm assessment of how welcoming both growing and baseline churches are to non-Christians, it may be that, when it comes to church growth, intentional discipleship/spiritual formation is more significant overall than hospitality.

EVANGELISM & OUTREACH

	CHURCH LEADERS		CONGREGATION	
	GROWING	BASELINE	GROWING	BASELINE
Q: HOW TRUE ARE EACH OF THE FOLLOWING STATEMENTS FOR YOUR CHURCH? (% COMPLETELY TRUE)				
The church teaches that evangelism is more than an event.	87%	30%	61%	42%
The congregation is encouraged to talk about their faith in Jesus with others.	78%	37%	63%	47%
Those who are not Christian feel welcome at this church.	65%	19%	38%	28%
Evangelism and discipleship are integrated, not isolated; those who accept Christ are consistently nurtured toward maturity.	48%	9%	---	---
The church sponsors outreach events designed to meet the needs of the local community.	44%	21%	56%	34%
The church provides outreach training.	17%	7%	26%	8%

6. SERVING & SOCIAL JUSTICE

For some churches, outreach and evangelism are deeply entwined with service and social justice programmes and activities. Is this an effective approach? Two-thirds of growing church leaders (65%), compared with half of baseline leaders (46%), link their engagement in social justice activities with successful outreach.

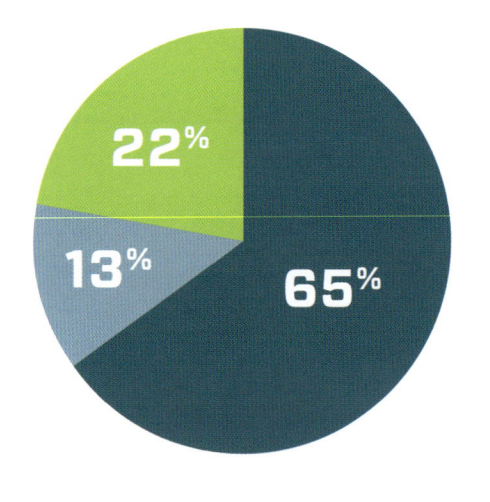

IMPACT OF SOCIAL JUSTICE ACTIVITIES ON SHARING THE GOSPEL: GROWING CHURCHES

% AMONG GROWING CHURCH LEADERS

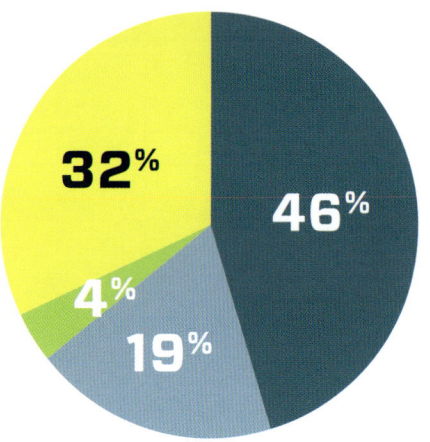

- POSITIVE — 65%
- NEITHER GOOD NOR BAD — 13%
- A DISTRACTION — 22%
- NOT SURE

IMPACT OF SOCIAL JUSTICE ACTIVITIES ON SHARING THE GOSPEL: BASELINE CHURCHES

% AMONG BASELINE CHURCH LEADERS

- POSITIVE — 46%
- NEITHER GOOD NOR BAD — 19%
- A DISTRACTION — 4%
- NOT SURE — 32%

Most churches—even growing ones—lack a strong commitment to serving outside the church. For example, fewer than half of people in growing churches say it is 'completely true' that serving outside the church is just as important as serving the needs of people within the church (48%); that is double the number of baseline churchgoers who say so (24%). Similarly, among growing church leaders only two-fifths say their church makes a priority of serving those outside the church (41%); among baseline leaders, about one in eight say the same (14%).

Barna discovered mixed results when we audited the types of programmes churches offer to their communities. To begin with, it is surprising that most growing and baseline churches say they do not have 'programmes in place at the church to support people in need in their local community': Just 27 per cent of growing church leaders and 11 per cent of baseline leaders report such a programme maintained by their community of faith. Few leaders place much emphasis on 'expanding people's comfort zones in outreach or community service'; only one-quarter of growing (23%) and one in 50 baseline leaders (2%) express this philosophy of community service.

Nonetheless, congregations claim relatively strong community engagement. When asked to identify ways in which they serve the community either as a church or as an individual, modest to strong levels of community service were reported (see chart below). Perhaps service efforts are sporadic or accomplished through third-party ministries or charities through which congregants volunteer.

The most common ways that churchgoers claim that their church is involved include serving local schools, supporting families and the elderly, and feeding the poor. Growing and baseline congregations report participation at similar levels in most activities, except when it comes to serving local schools and helping the elderly; in these, people in growing churches cite significantly greater involvement than those in baseline congregations.

ENGAGING IN SERVICE & SOCIAL JUSTICE

● BASELINE CHURCH CONGREGATIONS ● GROWING CHURCH CONGREGATIONS

HOW MY CHURCH ENGAGES — *HOW I ENGAGE*

Activity	Baseline (Church)	Growing (Church)	Baseline (I)	Growing (I)
feeding the poor	82%	69%	30%	28%
serving local schools	55%	91%	12%	20%
working to address extreme global poverty	46%	52%	23%	15%
addressing justice locally or nationally (such as homelessness and unemployment)	39%	55%	16%	24%

ENGAGING IN SERVICE & SOCIAL JUSTICE (CONT.)

● BASELINE CHURCH CONGREGATIONS   ● GROWING CHURCH CONGREGATIONS

HOW MY CHURCH ENGAGES / *HOW I ENGAGE*

Category	My Church: Baseline	My Church: Growing	I Engage: Baseline	I Engage: Growing
addressing justice internationally (such as child prostitution, trafficking, racism, sectarianism)	31%	34%	12%	13%
supporting and helping the elderly	40%	67%	19%	27%
supporting families	62%	75%	28%	40%
supporting mission partners overseas	97%	92%	41%	39%

7. PRAYER & WORSHIP

Life and ministry within growing churches appear to be more 'prayer-dependent' than is true among the norm of churches in Scotland. They claim to pray more specifically and more consistently than baseline leaders and members. However, there is room for improvement among both church types, especially when it comes to the authenticity and vitality of prayer.

    About six in 10 growing church leaders (57%) and members (59%) say that all significant ministry-related decisions are made prayerfully; significantly fewer baseline leaders (38%) and members (38%) say this is 'completely true' of their church. Growing churches are also more apt to pray specifically for the challenges of living faithfully in a post-Christian culture (55% leaders; 41% members, compared to one in five baseline leaders and members).

HABITS OF PRAYER

% 'COMPLETELY TRUE' AMONG GROWING AND BASELINE LEADERS AND CONGREGATIONS

- BASELINE CHURCH LEADERS
- BASELINE CHURCH MEMBERS
- GROWING CHURCH LEADERS
- GROWING CHURCH MEMBERS

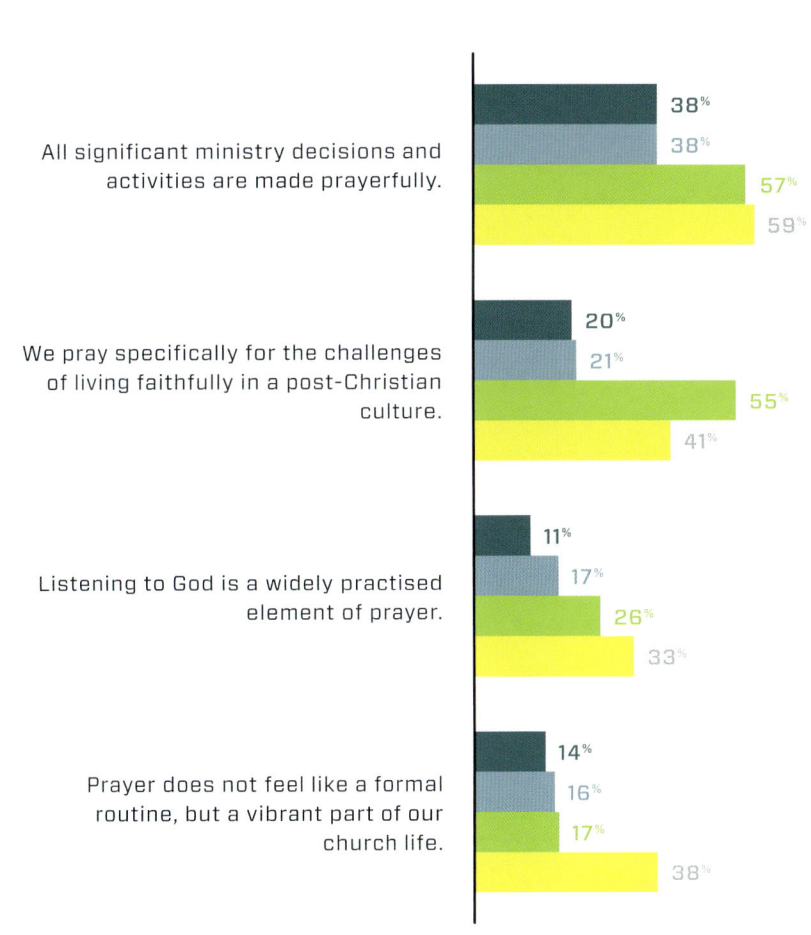

All significant ministry decisions and activities are made prayerfully.
- Baseline Church Leaders: 38%
- Baseline Church Members: 38%
- Growing Church Leaders: 57%
- Growing Church Members: 59%

We pray specifically for the challenges of living faithfully in a post-Christian culture.
- Baseline Church Leaders: 20%
- Baseline Church Members: 21%
- Growing Church Leaders: 55%
- Growing Church Members: 41%

Listening to God is a widely practised element of prayer.
- Baseline Church Leaders: 11%
- Baseline Church Members: 17%
- Growing Church Leaders: 26%
- Growing Church Members: 33%

Prayer does not feel like a formal routine, but a vibrant part of our church life.
- Baseline Church Leaders: 14%
- Baseline Church Members: 16%
- Growing Church Leaders: 17%
- Growing Church Members: 38%

More growing than baseline churches report that 'listening to God' is a widely practised prayer discipline, but proportions are low in every segment. More concerning are the fewer than one in six baseline leaders (14%), members (16%) and growing church leaders (17%) who say it is 'completely true' that 'prayer does not feel like a formal routine, but a vibrant part of our church life'. On a more positive note, nearly two out of five growing church members perceive prayer as a vibrant part of their church life (38%). This may indicate that members are learning and growing in relationship with the Lord more than their leaders comprehend.

Connecting with God in worship, perhaps even more than prayer, seems to characterise thriving churches. Seven in 10 growing church leaders report working diligently to grow the congregation's understanding of who God is through the worship experience (70%), twice that of baseline leaders (35%). They also remind people regularly that worship is a lifestyle, not merely an event (70%), more than double than among baseline leaders (29%). Interestingly, growing church members are less sanguine than their leaders on this question (50%), while baseline members are more confident than theirs (36%). While growing church leaders clearly intend to communicate the value of a worship lifestyle, fewer of their congregants are 'hearing' that message. However, growing church members and leaders both say it is 'completely true' that 'the worship focus is on connection with God, not on musical performance or sermon brilliance' (46% and 44%, respectively). Baseline leaders (27%) and members (35%) are less likely to say this is true of their church.

Leaders and members of both church categories disagree about how, exactly, to categorise the style of their worship services. About eight in 10 of each segment say 'modern' is an apt description of their worship style, but there is significant disparity on other descriptors such as 'liturgical', 'traditional (such as hymns)' and 'charismatic (that is, believing in the gifts of the spirit)'. A larger proportion of baseline churches report holding liturgical services, but overall, baseline and growing churches likely do not look remarkably different from the 'outside' when it comes to their worship services.

STYLES OF WORSHIP USED BY THE CHURCH

% AMONG GROWING AND BASELINE LEADERS AND CONGREGATIONS

- BASELINE CHURCH LEADERS
- BASELINE CHURCH MEMBERS
- GROWING CHURCH LEADERS
- GROWING CHURCH MEMBERS

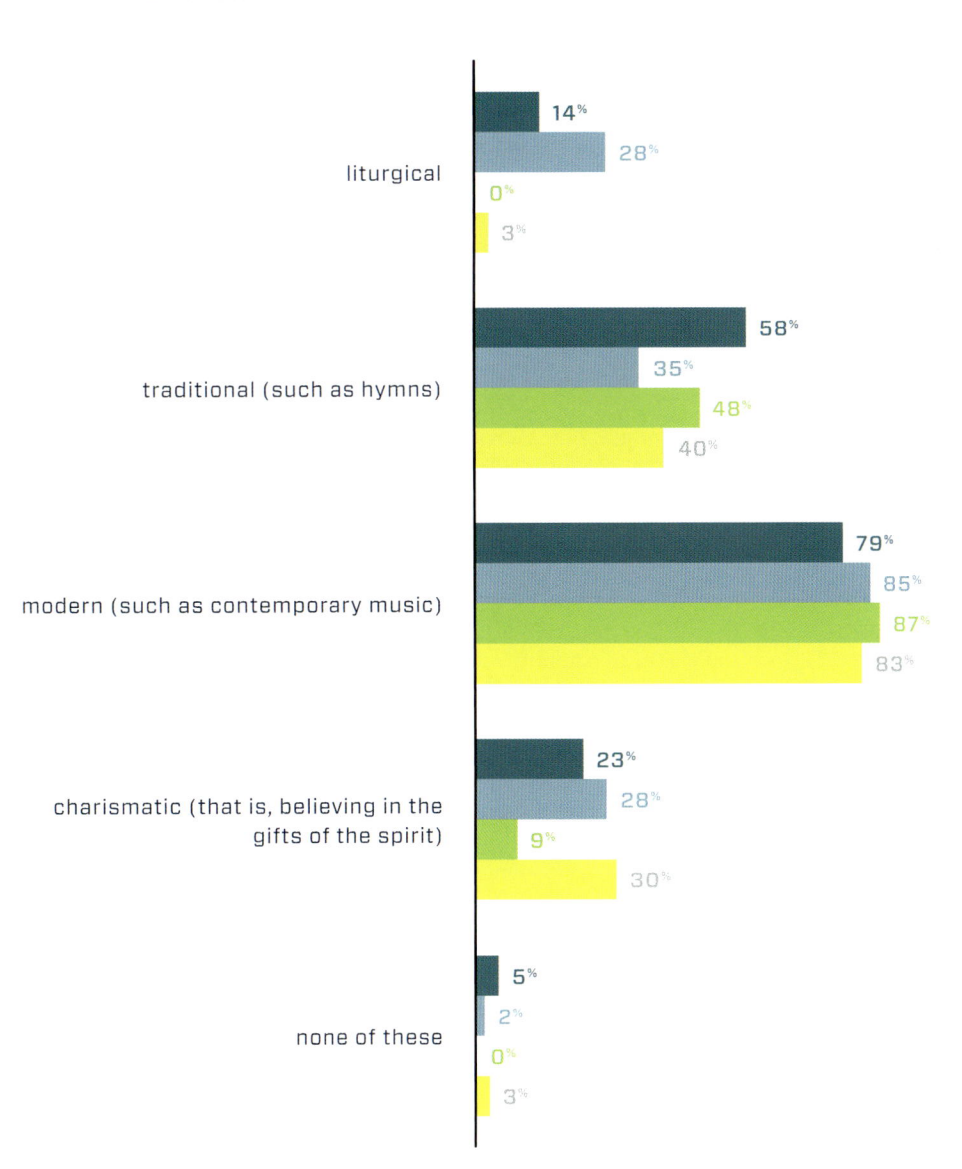

liturgical
- Baseline Church Leaders: 14%
- Baseline Church Members: 28%
- Growing Church Leaders: 0%
- Growing Church Members: 3%

traditional (such as hymns)
- Baseline Church Leaders: 58%
- Baseline Church Members: 35%
- Growing Church Leaders: 48%
- Growing Church Members: 40%

modern (such as contemporary music)
- Baseline Church Leaders: 79%
- Baseline Church Members: 85%
- Growing Church Leaders: 87%
- Growing Church Members: 83%

charismatic (that is, believing in the gifts of the spirit)
- Baseline Church Leaders: 23%
- Baseline Church Members: 28%
- Growing Church Leaders: 9%
- Growing Church Members: 30%

none of these
- Baseline Church Leaders: 5%
- Baseline Church Members: 2%
- Growing Church Leaders: 0%
- Growing Church Members: 3%

8. THEOLOGY & RELIGIOUS ACTIVITY

Barna's research on religious engagement and theological understanding shows that baseline and growing churches overlap in most ways. This suggests that growing churches do not merely have a substantively different, more active, membership than baseline churches. Something other than theology and religious practices is at work to stimulate and spur outstanding growth.

For example, when it comes to religious behaviours, such as attending a small group, sharing with a non-Christian about one's own faith or volunteering to serve in church or for another ministry, there is little difference between baseline and growing congregations. People who belong to both church types are equally likely to engage in these activities. Likewise, there is little significant difference between the groups when it comes to frequency of church attendance or Bible reading, and only minor differences when it comes to length of tenure at their present church (70 per cent of baseline churchgoers report attending their current church for eight or more years, compared to 62 per cent of people in growing churches).

Similar to religious activities, there is little daylight between the two groups when it comes to matters of theology. Growing church congregations are a bit more apt to agree strongly that 'the Bible is authoritative in all that it teaches' (80%, compared to 72% baseline) and that they have a personal responsibility to tell other people about their religious beliefs (71%, compared to 57% baseline). They are slightly more likely to prefer a literal understanding of the devil, or Satan, rather than believing he is merely a symbol of evil (disagree strongly 75%, compared to 63% baseline), and to believe that Jesus is actually returning to earth someday (91%, compared to 83% baseline).

Similarly, using Bebbington's four-part rubric, people in growing churches (84%) are only slightly more likely than baseline churchgoers (78%) to qualify as 'evangelical'. (Bebbington's rubric includes 'biblicism', 'crucicentrism', 'activism' and 'conversionism'. The Barna segmentation categories used to correlate with this rubric are detailed in Part I.) Those who belong to baseline congregations, meanwhile, are slightly more likely to qualify as 'non-evangelical born again', meaning that they report having confessed Jesus as Saviour and making a commitment to him that is still important in their life today—but do not otherwise meet the 'evangelical' qualifications.

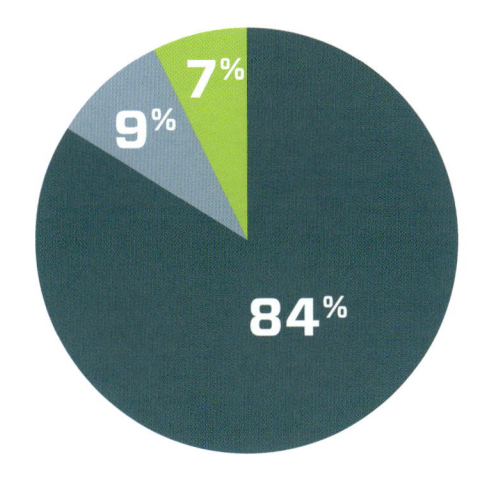

FAITH SEGMENTS: GROWING CHURCHES

% AMONG GROWING CHURCH CONGREGATIONS

- EVANGELICAL
- NON-EVANGELICAL BORN AGAIN
- OTHER

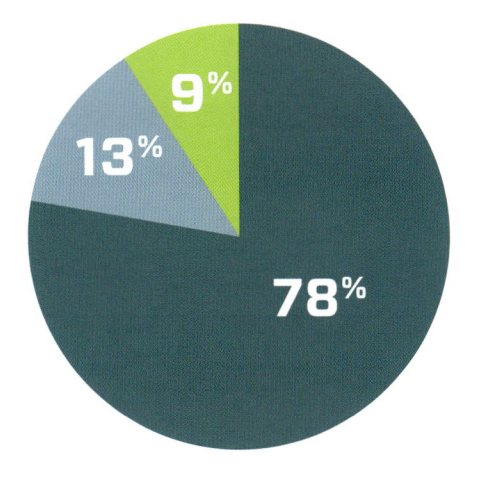

84%
9%
7%

FAITH SEGMENTS: BASELINE CHURCHES

% AMONG BASELINE CHURCH CONGREGATIONS

- EVANGELICAL
- NON-EVANGELICAL BORN AGAIN
- OTHER

78%
13%
9%

It is not surprising that baseline and growing churches are more similar than dissimilar on a majority of these measures of religious beliefs and behaviours. Most of these beliefs and practices, after all, represent a generally orthodox evangelicalism. More to the point, the data examined in this chapter suggest that generating a growing church is not merely a matter of finding more active, theologically orthodox members. Both growing and baseline churches are comprised of similar pools of people; the differences seem largely to be those of leadership, community and prayer.

9. STEWARDSHIP & VOCATION

When a biblical worldview permeates a church and its members, more than Bible knowledge and 'correct' theology are the result; people orient their lives around values that emanate from their worldview, in areas as diverse and practical as money management and career choices. This comprehensive worldview orientation may be a transformational key.

Growing churches appear to have a clear sense of God-centred resources. Substantial majorities (70% leaders; 60% congregation) say it is 'completely true' that, among their faith community, stewardship is understood 'to be the appropriate use of all the resources entrusted to us by God'. On a related point, two-thirds of growing church leaders (64%) and more than half of the people in their congregations (54%) confirm 'leaders teach that one's heart for investing God's resources is more important than giving a specific amount'.

Interestingly, not only are baseline churches lower overall than growing churches on these stewardship-related points, but leaders are even less likely than members to say these statements accurately describe their church. We cannot conclude the cause of this difference, but it may relate to a lack of confidence in their people, a greater sense of realism or less intentionality on the part of these leaders to teach biblical stewardship.

ATTITUDES ABOUT & PERSPECTIVES ON STEWARDSHIP

% 'COMPLETELY TRUE' AMONG GROWING AND BASELINE LEADERS AND CONGREGATIONS

- BASELINE CHURCH LEADERS
- BASELINE CONGREGATIONS
- GROWING CHURCH LEADERS
- GROWING CONGREGATIONS

Stewardship in my church is understood to be the appropriate use of all the resources entrusted to us by God.
- Baseline Church Leaders: 38%
- Baseline Congregations: 51%
- Growing Church Leaders: 70%
- Growing Congregations: 60%

Leaders teach that one's heart for investing God's resources is more important than giving a specific amount.
- Baseline Church Leaders: 27%
- Baseline Congregations: 39%
- Growing Church Leaders: 64%
- Growing Congregations: 54%

Work is another arena where one's worldview is manifested. Both growing (85%) and baseline congregations (88%) report a robust sense that 'all the work I do, whether paid or volunteer, is important to God'. They believe this even more strongly than their leaders report teaching it: Three-quarters of growing church leaders (74%) and nearly half of baseline leaders (45%) say they teach 'that all work is important to God'.

Similar proportions among the congregations disagree with the statement 'my faith and my work are two separate parts of my life' (63% growing; 55% baseline). Clearly, there is a sense among churchgoers that their faith and work should interconnect in a meaningful way. However, smaller proportions feel confident that they are making this connection, and that their faith community is helping them to do so. One-third of people in growing churches (35%) and one in five baseline churchgoers (19%) agree that 'the biblical teaching I receive at church is applicable to the issues and challenges I face in the workplace'. Similar proportions say it is 'completely true' that 'my church does a good job of helping me understand how to live out my faith in the workplace' (33% growing; 15% baseline).

This is not for lack of trying, according to their leaders: Half of growing church leaders (52%) and more than one-third of baseline leaders (36%) say they make a concerted effort to help congregants understand how to make the work-faith connection. Somewhat fewer leaders claim that 'we help people find fulfilment in their work by putting their God-given talents to work' (35% growing; 25% baseline)—a project that seems to have had more success, since 43 per cent of people in growing churches and 37 per cent of baseline churchgoers report they find fulfilment in their work by using their talents.

ATTITUDES ABOUT & PERSPECTIVES ON VOCATION

% 'COMPLETELY TRUE' AMONG GROWING AND BASELINE LEADERS AND CONGREGATIONS

- BASELINE CHURCH LEADERS
- BASELINE CONGREGATIONS
- GROWING CHURCH LEADERS
- GROWING CONGREGATIONS

Statement	Baseline Leaders	Baseline Congregations	Growing Leaders	Growing Congregations
All work is important to God.	45%	88%	74%	85%
Church helps people/me find fulfilment in work by using their/my God-given talents.	25%	37%	35%	43%
Church helps people/me understand how to live out faith in the workplace.	36%	15%	52%	33%

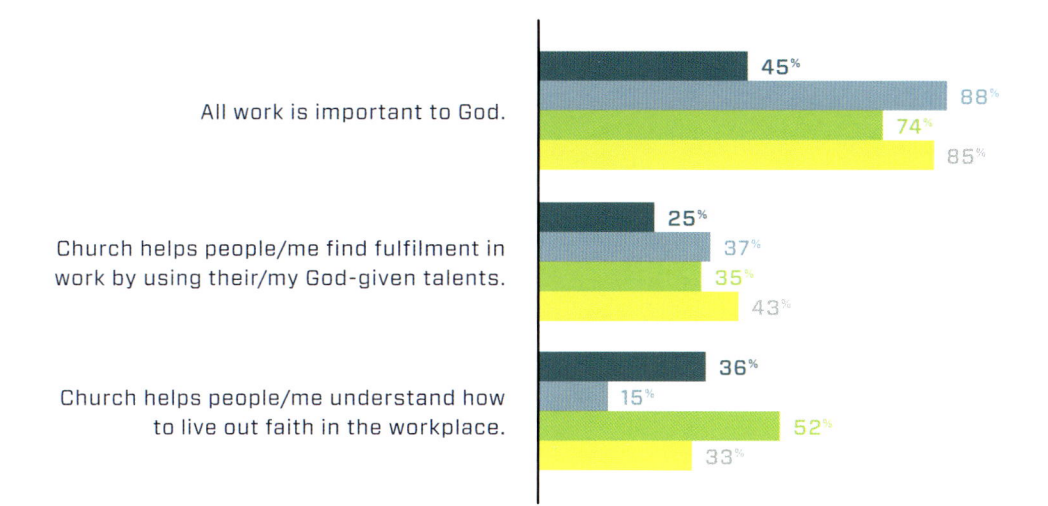

10. RESOURCES & PARTNERSHIPS

The final dimension of the study was an effort to pinpoint the organisations that are viewed as most beneficial to church leaders and their congregations. The survey question asked respondents to identify the groups that have been most helpful to their church/spiritual growth in the past year.

Respondents were asked, without prompting or a list of options, to name the organisation that has been most helpful. This research method is called 'unaided awareness', and the goal is to elicit the answer that is 'top of mind'. When it comes to unaided awareness, church leaders are most likely to name the following organisations as most helpful:

1. Scripture Union (16%)
2. Alpha (12%)
3. Tearfund (10%)
4. Church of Scotland (8%, tie)
5. Messy Church (8%, tie)
6. Spring Harvest (8%, tie)

Unaided, congregation members identify the following as most helpful:

1. Alpha (21%)
2. 3DM (15%)
3. Scripture Union (13%)
4. Christians Against Poverty (8%)
5. Glasgow City Mission (5%, tie)
6. Tearfund (5%, tie)

Notice in the following table that only about 20 groups or ministries generated two per cent or more responses among leaders; only about 13 organisations prompted two per cent or more awareness among churchgoers. Scores of organisations—shown as 'other'—were identified by fewer than one per cent of respondents. We might call these results 'fragmented', since there is not a consensus of awareness about any single organisation.

ORGANISATION HELPFULNESS: UNAIDED AWARENESS

	CHURCH LEADERS	CONGRE-GATION		CHURCH LEADERS	CONGRE-GATION
Alpha	12%	21%	Care for the Family	6%	NA
3DM	4%	15%	Barnabas Fund	6%	NA
Scripture Union	16%	13%	Crieff Fellowship	6%	NA
CAP – Christians Against Poverty	NA	8%	Cornhill	6%	NA
Glasgow City Mission	4%	5%	Street Pastors	4%	NA
Tearfund	10%	5%	Biblical Counseling / CCEF	4%	NA
Bethany Christian Trust	NA	4%	Guild	4%	NA
Church of Scotland	8%	4%	Bethel	2%	NA
Catalyst	NA	4%	don't know	10%	20%
OM	NA	4%	other*	47%	53%
CLAN	6%	3%			
LICC	4%	3%			
Baptist Union	4%	3%			
Messy Church	8%	NA			
Spring Harvest	8%	NA			
Christianity Explored	6%	NA			

* includes organisations mentioned by 1% or fewer respondents

Fragmentation among evangelical churches and organisations extends, as well, to local outreach partnerships. In this, growing and baseline leaders report a similar record: About one-third say it is 'completely' or 'mostly true' that 'the church regularly cooperates in outreach activities with other nearby churches or organisations'. (Anecdotally, the researchers have been informed that churches are more likely to partner with others on training than on outreach, but the study was designed only to assess outreach partnerships.)

The fact that growing churches are so similar to baseline churches in this regard, and the fact that only about one-eighth of church leaders say it is 'completely true' that they cooperate regularly in effective outreach partnerships, suggests that Scottish churches are struggling to form and sustain such relationships. In other words, most congregations tend to operate solo when it comes to outreach, rather than in concert with the broader Body of Christ.

CHURCH PARTNERS IN OUTREACH WITH OTHER LOCAL MINISTRIES ON A REGULAR BASIS

% AMONG GROWING AND BASELINE CHURCH LEADERS

● COMPLETELY TRUE ● MOSTLY TRUE ● SOMEWHAT TRUE ● NOT MUCH ● NOT AT ALL

	Completely True	Mostly True	Somewhat True	Not Much	Not At All
growing church leaders	13%	22%	39%	22%	4%
baseline church leaders	14%	19%	39%	18%	11%

WHAT'S WORKING AMONG MILLENNIALS?

Three themes emerged from the Millennials-focused research as key factors in helping Millennials stay committed to church and to Jesus. Millennials who are developing a deeply rooted faith consistently point to these factors as critical to their spiritual growth—at significantly higher rates than their congregations as a whole.

1. MEANINGFUL & AUTHENTIC RELATIONSHIPS
2. DEEP UNDERSTANDING OF FAITH
3. OPPORTUNITIES TO SERVE OTHERS

●●● MILLENNIALS   ● CONGREGATIONAL TOTALS

1. MEANINGFUL & AUTHENTIC RELATIONSHIPS

I find the Bible most useful when I discuss it with others.
- 72%
- 57%

The church is a place where I belong.
- 67%
- 57%

I have access to leadership training at church.
- 50%
- 37%

2. DEEP UNDERSTANDING OF FAITH

Sermons in my church offer both biblical principles and life application.
- 67%
- 53%

The Bible teaching I receive at my church is relevant to my life.
- 56%
- 47%

My church does a good job of helping me understand how to live out my faith in the workplace.
- 36%
- 26%

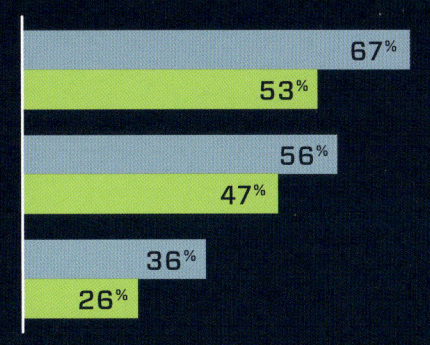

3. OPPORTUNITIES TO SERVE OTHERS

My church is involved in addressing justice internationally.
- 50%
- 35%

My church is involved in addressing justice locally or nationally.
- 65%
- 49%

In the past 30 days, I have volunteered free time to help my church.
- 90%
- 82%

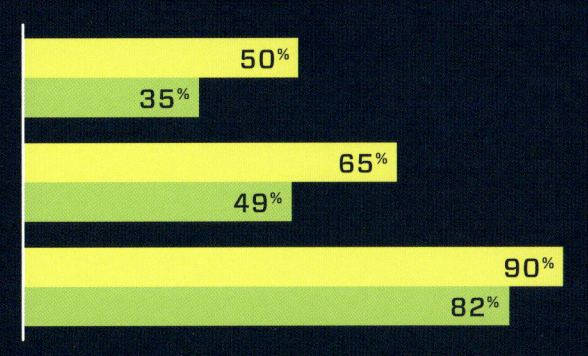

PART III
MILLENNIALS STUDY

Concurrent with the launch of the best practices study, the researchers commenced a study of Scottish Millennials, ages 18 to 30, who are involved in congregations and parachurch ministries. This effort was designed to further assess the clear indicators presented by the survey of the general population: that many Millennial Scots are expressing renewed interest in the Bible and in Christianity. This is one of the bright spots uncovered by the research: Generational loss of faith does not seem to be a foregone conclusion. The strategic question is, what can be learned about Millennials that can help church leaders to move with and augment this countertrend?

The research generated 103 completed responses from Millennials. Across the entire study, the Barna team has interviewed more than 300 Millennials. Although the religious landscape continues to shift, a small but notable group of Scottish Millennials has emerged as faith leaders among their generation. Using both qualitative and quantitative research methods, we have identified several factors that distinguish them from their age cohort and from Scottish Christians at large. These factors likely contribute to the ability of these Millennials to grow into spiritual maturity and leadership capacities that are desperately needed among their generation.

Because the research in this section is based on findings from two groups of Millennials, they are distinguished in the text as 'congregational Millennials' (Millennial respondents to the congregational study) and 'engaged Millennials' (Millennials who are actively engaged in faith and were asked both qualitative and quantitative questions). Congregational Millennials are compared to the total percentages across growing and baseline churches, since the Millennial respondents were drawn from both church cohorts.

THEMES

Three themes emerged from the Millennials-focused research: meaningful and authentic relationships, relevant understanding of faith and opportunities to serve others. We discovered that these factors help Millennials stay committed to church and to Jesus. Statistics that support these themes are drawn from the congregational study, and the findings compare the total congregation (growing and baseline) with the Millennial subset.

Meaningful & Authentic Relationships

- I find the Bible most useful when I discuss it with others. (Millennials, 72%; congregational total, 52%)
- The church is a place where I belong. (Millennials, 67%; congregational total, 57%)
- The change that would make the most difference to the health and influence of the church in Scotland would be outward focus, evangelism and relationship building with nonbelievers. (Millennials, 16%; congregational total, 8%)

For Millennials who are developing a deeply rooted faith, one consistent trend is that they have leaders or mentors in their church community from whom they can learn and ask questions. When asked about specific catalysts for spiritual growth in their personal life, one Millennial shared the following:

> *Many approachable male leaders in the church, who have been willing to have a chat about anything on any short notice, and especially who model their fears, worries, insecurities and inadequacies, but only in conjunction with GOD's transforming and redeeming work in their lives (i.e. what are their struggles, but how GOD fixes stuff), in a way that points me away from idolizing and aspiring to BE them, but towards being LIKE them in submission to Christ.*

This response is a rich example of how meaningful relationships are a fruitful way for Millennials to grow into spiritual maturity. Specifically, the leaders identified in this quote exhibit the following qualities: approachability, openness, availability, vulnerability, readiness to communicate and God-centredness. The impact of these characteristics generated a catalytic effect on this young man's faith journey.

In addition to relationships that are deep and authentic, engaged Millennials also have access to leadership training at church: In the congregational study, 50 per cent of Millennials report receiving leadership training from their church, compared to 37 per cent of the total. Not only do they have access to training, but they also have access to *excellent* training. Among the half of Millennials who had received any leadership training from their church, 50 per cent report that the training they received was 'excellent', with a combined total of only 6 per cent reporting it was 'inadequate' or 'poor'. Opportunities for leadership training and relational development are tangible ways that churches can invest in Millennials and equip them with essential tools (relational, spiritual and practical) to strengthen both their personal faith and the whole church.

Although these engaged Millennials are now receiving training and mentoring from their churches, the research also found that a limited number of them received that kind of support in secondary school. When asked if they had had an adult mentor at church, other than the pastor or staff, during secondary school only 28 per cent of Millennials said yes. It is also notable that, among those who were mentored, young men were twice as likely as young women to have been mentored during secondary school (44% of men compared to 19% of women). This suggests that, fortunately, Millennials are often mentored later in their lives (post-secondary school), but that there is also an enormous opportunity to invest in younger members of Christ's Body as they grow up.

The research shows that, for engaged Millennials, faith-based relationships are consistently a priority. Among these committed Millennials, 84 per cent say the statement 'I think going to church or being with Christian friends is optional' is 'not at all true' of them (indicating that they understand faith-centred relationships as essential). Rejection of self-contained spirituality is a powerful indicator of the Millennial countertrend, and is important to actively churched Millennials.

Deep Understanding of Faith
- [In my church] sermons consistently offer both biblical principles and life application. (Millennials, 67%; congregational total, 53%)
- The Bible teaching I receive in my church is relevant to my life. (Millennials, 56%; congregational total, 47%)
- My church does a good job of helping me to understand how to live out my faith in the workplace. (Millennials, 36%; congregational total, 26%)

Although deep relationships and mentoring can strengthen the foundation of Millennials' faith, that same faith can wither if it is not clear to them how it is relevant to their lives and cultural context. In a society that encourages sensory and superficial experiences, Millennials will pass by church teachings and community if there is no direct application. In one in-depth interview, one young adult articulated how this challenge is unique to their generation:

[It is a] challenge to see how Jesus is Lord over the whole of life. Often my generation has been taught glib soundbites and gospel outlines rather than developing deep convictions and a knowledge of the person of Jesus. This lack of depth is then reinforced by an aversion to Bible reading or doing anything that takes longer than five minutes! And results in shaky faith that is easily rocked because it's not really built on anything firm and bears no relevance to the rest of life.

Another committed Millennial explained:

I think there is an overwhelming amount of apathy or disregard in matters of faith and church involvement within my generation because many seem to not care enough about it to try and understand why it is important.

As these responses indicate, an ability to deeply understand faith concepts and overcome distraction is a key signifier of committed Christian Millennials. When faith is deeply rooted and personal, Millennials can withstand the barrage of narratives that attempt to undermine their worldview. Yet in a world where the digital and social landscapes are fraught with 'soundbites' of religious information, it is difficult for Scottish Millennials to cultivate a spiritual life with this depth.

Another marker of engaged Millennials is how they see the Bible: as an indispensable guide to navigating today's complex world. Fifty-six per cent say it is 'completely true' that the Bible teaching they receive in their church is relevant to their life. The remaining proportion of Millennials—44 per cent—say the statement is 'mostly true', meaning that every young adult we interviewed reports receiving relevant Bible teaching from their church. The frequency with which these Millennial Christians read the Bible is also high: 96 per cent report reading the Bible at least once a week; 52 per cent read several times a week; and 20 per cent read every day.

Discussing the Bible with others is one key way that engaged Millennials grow in appreciation for Scripture. When asked to identify settings in which the Bible is most useful, 72 per cent say, 'When I discuss it with others' (about half of the total congregational study selected this answer). This finding highlights the relational and communal bent of today's Millennial Scots. In discussing the Bible with others, Millennials are forced to engage with their own personal feelings about the Bible. When Millennials are committed to the study and application of the Bible in their own lives, these interactions are even more powerful because they're happening in in the context of relationships.

Deeply rooted Millennials also feel safe to ask tough questions in their churches. Of the Millennial Christians we surveyed, 60 per cent say it is 'not at all true' that they 'can't ask my most pressing life questions in church'. All together, almost seven out of 10 committed Christian Millennials have relatively high levels of comfort asking difficult questions in church. Not only is this an indicator that their churches are open to any question, but also that, by asking their questions, engaged Millennials have developed trust in their church communities.

For Millennials engaged with the church, faith is something that they understand as central to their lives. And not only is it a centralising force, but it also fits into their larger understanding of how they see themselves and the world. Almost all of the Christian Millennials we surveyed say that the statement 'Christian beliefs just don't make sense to me' does not at all describe them (92%). When a Millennial can understand the relevance of a Christian worldview to their own life and context, it gives them a broader sense of purpose for how faith fits into every corner of their lives. One Millennial shared about his or her most catalytic growth points:

Attending a Jesus-centred church. Spending time in a small group, learning from others and the Bible. Realising my faith is the most important thing that I do.

Many engaged Millennial Christians began to explore a deeper understanding of faith from a young age. During secondary school, 56 per cent learned to view their gifts and passions as a part of God's calling, and 40 per cent better understood their purpose in life through church. Additionally during this time, 48 per cent learned about how Christians can positively contribute to society. While the researchers maintain the view that Millennials who are disconnected from the church represent an enormous opportunity for the Scottish church, it is clear from these interviews that a solid foundation for healthy spiritual development is often laid early in life. Effective, disciple-making youth ministries must continue to be at the forefront of this effort.

Opportunities to Serve Others

- My church is involved in addressing justice internationally. (Millennials, 50%; congregational total, 35%)
- My church is involved in addressing justice locally or nationally. (Millennials, 65%; congregational total, 49%)
- In the past 30 days I have volunteered free time to help my church. (Millennials, 90%; congregational total, 82%)

Another factor that helps engaged Millennials grow in faith is having plentiful opportunities to serve, both spiritually and tangibly. In our qualitative research, one young adult shared an example of when they saw people in their church put their faith info effective action: 'My friend's daughter is critically ill in hospital, at the same time their newborn had arrived. I've seen the church gather around them in prayer and practical help.'

The serving opportunities provided by this church are meeting both spiritual and physical needs. Yet, as the next anecdote from a Millennial illustrates, sometimes meeting a physical need can be a form of evangelism in and of itself: 'After the daughter of one person at church died tragically, many people provided meals for the family during their grief, which caused others in their family to start coming to church.'

It is interesting to note that, although many Millennials gave examples of service both local and international, isolated acts of evangelism were never mentioned as examples of putting faith into effective action. While we cannot speculate about why that is the case, we can say that seeing and participating in tangible service is an important way Millennials know their faith makes a difference in the world.

Compared to Christians of other generations, the engaged Millennials we surveyed are much more oriented toward justice efforts both locally and globally. When asked about what types of outreach engagement their current church is involved in, Millennials were more likely to report their church is involved internationally: 50 per cent of Millennials say their church is addressing justice outside of Scotland, compared to 35 per cent of all respondents. Two-thirds report their church is addressing justice locally or nationally. Millennials have grown up in the most connected world that humankind has ever experienced, so it's not a surprise that their passion for justice issues is both local and global. Opportunities to serve in multiple locales can help young adults put their beliefs into faith action.

RECOMMENDATIONS FOR REACHING MILLENNIALS

The following are suggestions for how to implement meaningful relationships, cultivation of deep faith and service opportunities into a church's outreach to Millennials. Every faith community is different, and these ideas are not exhaustive; other strategies may work better for your context.

To develop meaningful and authentic relationships:
- Create opportunities and/or programmes for Millennials to be mentored by other church members.
- Initiate meaningful relationships with youth as early as possible, and continue as Millennials transition into adulthood.
- Church members who mentor or invest in Millennials should be vulnerable, God-centred and open to answering difficult questions.
- Provide training to give Millennials the spiritual and tangible skills they need to lead others into deeper faith.
- Teach youth (secondary school and younger) that a healthy faith life can't be had absent a faith community.

To cultivate deep understanding and personal faith:
- Provide Millennials with resources and spaces to cultivate a thoughtful spiritual life. Some examples of this could be Bible reading plans, prayer retreats and outreach activities.
- Increase the number of opportunities for Millennials to discuss the Bible with others and possibly to teach others, as well.
- Clearly and explicitly communicate to Millennials that you are open to discussing any questions they have about faith and its role in their lives. Ideally, identify congregational leaders who also can be approached for questions and discussion.
- Include practical application or other real-life connection in every sermon, Bible study or teaching.

To offer opportunities to serve others:
- When serving people in your own church and community, meet both spiritual and physical/tangible needs.
- Invite Millennials to participate in serving others in your community and at your church. Ideally, identify their gifts and skills, and help them find ways to deploy these in service to others.
- Identify justice issues (locally, nationally and internationally) that your church can support and engage in with Millennials.

The three Millennial growth strategies—meaningful relationships, a relevant understanding of faith matters and opportunities to serve—strongly parallel the recommendations in 'Part IV. Implications & Recommendations'. Here are some specific ways that the findings on Scottish Millennials intersect with several of those recommendations.

The first overall recommendation, multiply leaders, is connected in a rather obvious way to Barna's findings about Millennials. Young adults will begin, over the next decade, to step into church leadership positions, so understanding what is working to develop current Millennial leaders is essential to effectively raise up the next generation of church leaders in Scotland.

Taking risks on entrepreneurial leaders can be achieved, in part, by looking to spiritually mature Millennials for guidance on how to create new church models that allow the gospel to penetrate the lives of communities and individuals. Scotland's church history is rooted in tradition and ritual, and the creative energy of younger adults can help transform this legacy into tools that build the Scottish church of today and of the future.

The active engagement of Scottish Millennial Christians with the Bible supports the fourth recommendation, teach the whole Bible for whole-life transformation. Although this recommendation primarily highlights the need to build church communities that are Bible-centred, the findings about Scottish Millennials also suggest that any Bible teaching must be offered in ways that are relevant to the audience. Integrating the Bible more into church life is only the first step; Millennials and other people in the congregation must understand how its wisdom applies to their own lives, or growth and spiritual transformation will likely be exceedingly difficult.

The findings detailed in this short section on engaged Millennials give specific strategies to accomplish the eighth recommendation, leverage the surprising trends among Millennials. Scottish Millennials are atypically open to faith, Jesus and the Bible, and the tools of relationship, relevant faith and service are all practical ways to develop this opportunity. Millennial church leaders themselves are prime candidates to lead this endeavor, since they can leverage their peer-to-peer status while relying on a solid foundation of faith (personal and communal) to support their efforts.

9 DRIVERS OF TRANSFORMATIVE MINISTRY

Analysing the findings from each phase of research, Barna Group identified nine key factors that can catalyse transformative ministry.

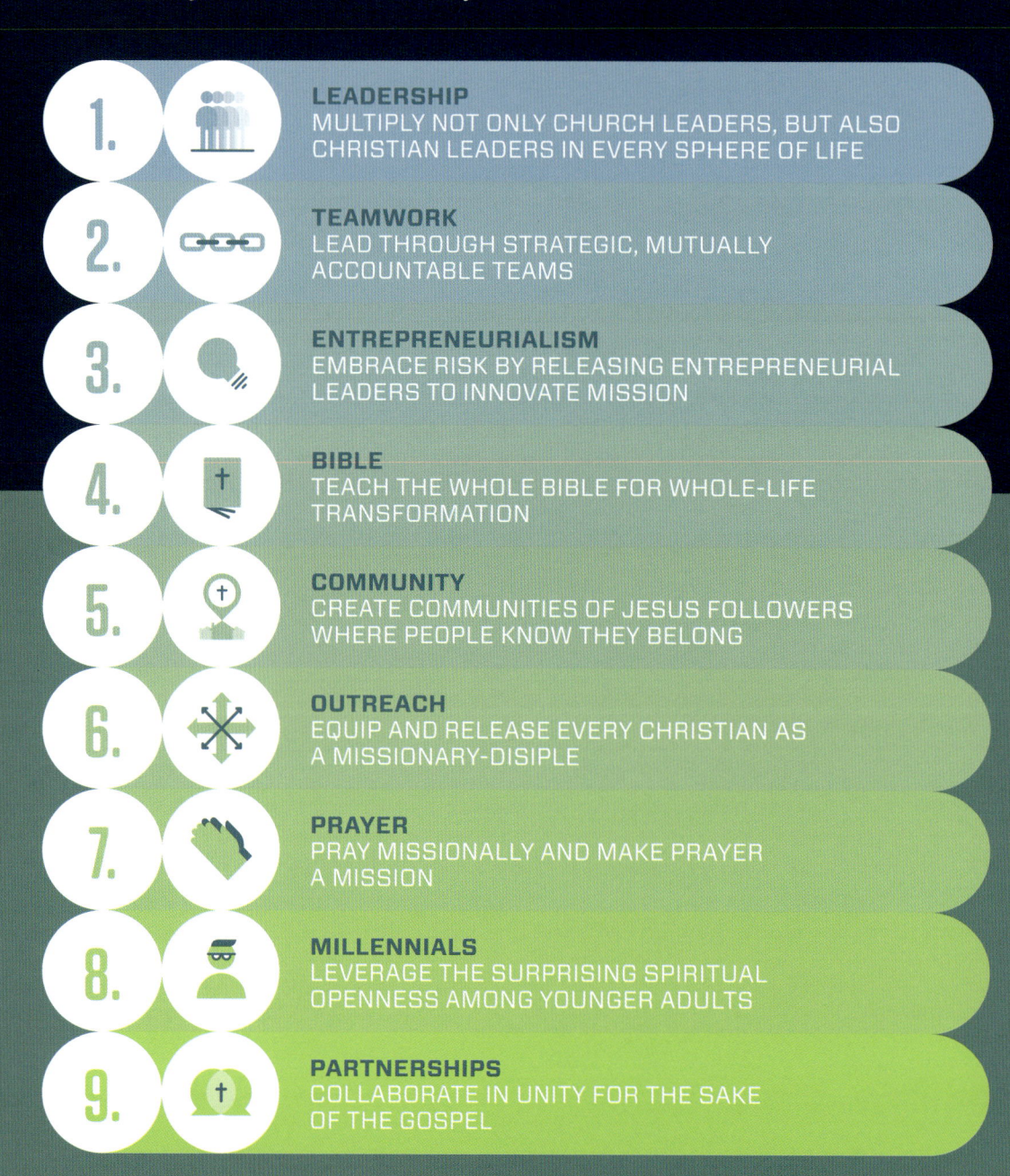

1. **LEADERSHIP**
MULTIPLY NOT ONLY CHURCH LEADERS, BUT ALSO CHRISTIAN LEADERS IN EVERY SPHERE OF LIFE

2. **TEAMWORK**
LEAD THROUGH STRATEGIC, MUTUALLY ACCOUNTABLE TEAMS

3. **ENTREPRENEURIALISM**
EMBRACE RISK BY RELEASING ENTREPRENEURIAL LEADERS TO INNOVATE MISSION

4. **BIBLE**
TEACH THE WHOLE BIBLE FOR WHOLE-LIFE TRANSFORMATION

5. **COMMUNITY**
CREATE COMMUNITIES OF JESUS FOLLOWERS WHERE PEOPLE KNOW THEY BELONG

6. **OUTREACH**
EQUIP AND RELEASE EVERY CHRISTIAN AS A MISSIONARY-DISIPLE

7. **PRAYER**
PRAY MISSIONALLY AND MAKE PRAYER A MISSION

8. **MILLENNIALS**
LEVERAGE THE SURPRISING SPIRITUAL OPENNESS AMONG YOUNGER ADULTS

9. **PARTNERSHIPS**
COLLABORATE IN UNITY FOR THE SAKE OF THE GOSPEL

PART IV
IMPLICATIONS & RECOMMENDATIONS

BEST PRACTICES CONCLUSIONS

What did we learn from the assessment of growing churches, described in Part II? Again, remember that Barna Group's goal was not to categorise some churches as better than others. Rather, we wanted to uncover factors that seem to contribute to better-than-average growth. If these churches are experiencing categorically different and more holistic expansion, their 'best practices' may offer clues to the transformation of hearts and minds of Scottish adults, and thus help revitalise Christianity in the nation. We believe these insights, if applied with discretion and prayer, can make investment and development of ministry more strategic and enduring.

We look first at best practices among leaders, then at best practices among congregations.

Best Practices of Growing Church Leaders
There are a number of overall insights that emerge from the best practices study. First, let's look at the biggest gaps between the leaders of growing churches and the leaders of baseline churches and what these differences imply. Remember: These differences are not necessarily causal, but the strength of the correlations lead us to identify six implications.

1. A healthy leadership culture makes a measurable difference.
The most common set of differences between the two groups of leaders who participated in the survey is growing leaders' emphasis on leader accountability, followed closely by their priority on leadership preparation. Out of the 20 largest gaps between growing and baseline leaders, fully half of the significant distinctions relate to leadership.

Interestingly, a premium on leadership accountability is even more likely than training to distinguish the leaders of growing churches. This includes such factors as 'teacher and facilitator training and evaluation are high priorities'; 'my ability to lead is regularly evaluated by other leaders'; and 'leaders promote and practise mutual accountability'.

The difference between growing and baseline church leaders is not a matter of motivation or passion for Jesus. The most significant difference seems to lie in growing church leaders' ability to think and act like true leaders in the context of a healthy leadership culture. This underscores the importance of not only providing leadership training, but also of identifying and unleashing called, competent and high-character leaders.

2. Equipping people to share their faith is a clear priority of growing church leaders.
Another common theme in the profile of growing church leaders is their emphasis on evangelism outreach. Growing churches are significantly more likely to offer evangelism training, to describe 'outreach' as more than just events, to create a welcoming environment for non-Christians and to intentionally integrate evangelism with discipleship and spiritual formation.

3. Growing church leaders teach the Bible systematically.
A third theme is the priority growing churches place on teaching the Bible in an expository or systematic way. They are committed to teaching the Bible clearly and thoroughly, exegeting both the biblical text and the culture where they and their people must apply Scripture's wisdom. They also seem to evaluate the success of their teaching based on evidence of life transformation, not merely 'head knowledge'.

4. Growing church leaders pray strategically.
Intentional, strategic prayer is also a common differentiator between growing church leaders and the norm in Scotland. A majority of growing church leaders says that significant leadership and ministry decisions are made only after prayer. Interestingly, the biggest prayer-related gap between the two types of churches is that growing churches report praying specifically for the challenges of living faithfully in a post-Christian culture. There seems to be an intentional, culturally aware manner of praying that defines growing churches.

5. Growing church leaders view deep, meaningful relationships as a vital aspect of ministry.
Growing church leaders seem to be keenly aware of the relational deficits experienced by many Scottish adults, families and children (deficits uncovered in Barna's review of secondary research). Growing

church leaders are distinctive in their desire to 'build honest and deep relationships with one another' and are also more likely than the norm to say their church has a strong and healthy ministry to families.

6. Growing church leaders prioritise serving the surrounding community.
While only a minority of growing church leaders in Scotland expresses this view, one of the biggest gaps between growing and baseline leaders is a desire to expand the congregation's comfort zones through outreach and community service (23% vs. 2% 'completely true', respectively). Another top-20 gap in this regard is having programmes in place to support people with needs in their local community. It should be noted that this emphasis on outreach defines many, though not all, growing churches. It seems to be important, but not a non-negotiable (as is the case with leadership, for example).

Best Practices of Growing Church Congregations
The previous six insights emerge from an examination of the leader data. Another way to analyse best practices for mission and ministry is to look at the gaps between the two different types of congregations. In other words, what are the biggest differences between growing and baseline churchgoers who completed the survey, and what do these differences indicate or imply? The researchers focused scrutiny on the 20 widest gaps between the two groups to determine if their profiles could provide clarifying insights into what is helping to transform lives.

1. Growing church congregations practise a priority on prayer.
First, in looking at the top differences between congregations, one of the major themes is, again, prayer. Even more so than among leaders, people who belong to growing churches are defined by their practice of and priority on prayer. Nearly one-third of the top differences between the two cohorts relate to this factor. These include a significant emphasis not only on formal prayer events, but also on making prayer a 'vibrant part of church life'; praying specifically for the 'challenges of living in a post-Christian culture'; and 'listening to God as a widely practised element of prayer' among the church community.

2. Growing church congregations value high-impact, knowledgeable leaders.
The research among churchgoers confirms that leadership is an important priority for people in growing churches. Interestingly, while leadership accountability is a key theme among the leaders themselves, people in growing churches tend more to care about leadership training and preparation.

3. Growing church congregations integrate faith with life.
People in growing churches tend to see faith integration as an important part of their church experience. For example, they are twice as likely as the norm to say they receive Bible teaching that is relevant to their lives. They are more than two times more likely than baseline churchgoers to say their church does a good job helping them to understand how to live out their faith in the workplace.

4. Growing church congregations are outwardly oriented.
People in growing churches are more likely than their fellow believers in baseline churches to say that their faith community prepares them for evangelism, and to say their church expands their comfort zones in outreach and community service. In other words, there seems to be an outward orientation that people in growing churches notice, appreciate and respond to.

THE TENSION BETWEEN REALITY AND HOPE

Taking into account the breadth of findings from this yearlong study, we must maintain the tension between two perspectives that, at first glance, seem difficult to hold in tandem. We must face Scotland's present reality with sober-mindedness and, at the same time, look to the future with trust and hope.

One of the most important conclusions from this research is that Christianity in Scotland is in a very serious condition. There is no getting around the fact that the Christian community has seen better days. Many challenges face churches, church leaders and Christian ministries, not the least of which is that forward momentum seems stalled. This report describes many of those challenges in 'Part I: The State of Faith in Scotland'.

While these facts are sobering, the second major conclusion is good news, indeed: There are reasons to be hopeful about the future of Christianity in Scotland. These include the following:

- The presence of more than 800,000 Scots—17 per cent of the population—who report they have confessed Jesus as Saviour and have made a commitment to him that is still important in their life today—even though nearly half of them do not currently attend church
- The ongoing, tireless efforts of thousands of gospel-centred churches and leaders in Scotland to impact their community with the gospel
- The overall optimism that church leaders, key influencers and especially younger pastors have about the possibility of spiritual renewal
- The fact that many young Scots (ages 18 to 30) seem to represent a countertrend—that is, there is resurgent interest in the Bible, in churchgoing and in Jesus among the Millennial generation of Scots
- The ongoing work of the Holy Spirit in the world and in the people of Scotland

RECOMMENDATIONS FOR TRANSFORMING SCOTLAND

We conclude this report with strategic imperatives that should guide future efforts to transform Scotland. As the Steering Group requested at the initiation of this project, Barna recommends the following 'guardrails' or 'guidelines' for evaluating where and how to invest in Scotland mission and ministry. The scope of this research was not designed to endorse specific ministries, churches, leaders or organisations for financial investment or other support. However, we believe the following strategies can reliably guide planning, decisions and investments.

1. Multiply leaders.
By far, one of the most significant findings from both the best practices study and the in-depth interviews with key influencers is the singular importance of developing leaders—not only clergy, but lay leaders in every sphere of Scottish life. Potential leaders need to be identified, trained, developed and then placed in positions with effective teams and biblical accountability. In many ways, investment in leaders is the first and most important priority, because these God-given and -gifted leaders will mobilise, motivate, equip and direct God's people to accomplish his vision for the church in Scotland.

2. Lead through strategic, mutually accountable teams.
Another strategic imperative for the Christian community in Scotland is to create a new leadership culture that relies on teams with complementary gifts and mutual accountability. Growing churches depend on a team of leaders, rather than only one 'lone-wolf' leader, to challenge, sharpen and support one another. The same is needed in the wider Scottish church. The New Testament church offers various models of plural leadership, and churches and organisations that hope to grow today must consider adopting such an approach.

3. Embrace risk by releasing entrepreneurial leaders to innovate mission.
Based on the national survey of Scottish adults, the current model of church in Scotland does not resonate with the vast majority of people. As such, ways of 'doing' and 'being' church will need to change in order to bring the Good News of Jesus to people to whom 'church' does not sound like good news. Determining the shape of these new expressions of church will likely demand a high tolerance for risk-taking and, quite possibly, failure as visionaries look beyond existing, tried-and-true structures. As the Christian community identifies and equips new leaders, and helps them form strategic teams of other gifted leaders, their visions for 'new wineskins' will be essential for the future of the church in Scotland.

4. Teach the whole Bible for whole-life transformation.
Another major theme emerging from the research is the primacy of cultivating a passion for and robust engagement with Scripture. In growing churches, leaders exegete the Bible and 'exegete' culture—that is, they help people to understand how God's Word, written by ancient people in alien cultures, applies today to their Scottish lives, families, friends and workplaces in Scottish communities. Leaders may need fresh biblical insights, coaching on how to apply Scripture to their current context and guidance on how to communicate these ideas more effectively. Likewise, church communities may need resources that guide them in how to read, interpret and apply the Bible.

5. Create communities of Jesus followers where people know they belong.
There is no single strategy that will guarantee Christianity's advance in Scotland; however, if the church is to thrive, it must be grounded in a powerful relational ethic, a countercultural expression of communal life. As Barna found in the review of secondary research, many Scots are lonely and stressed, and have fewer social, familial and relational bonds. Ironically, the digital age has both enhanced the ability to stay connected and has increased capacity for isolation. In contrast, people in growing churches seem to experience a powerful sense of belonging, acceptance and love. Consider how to nurture transparency and authenticity within existing congregations; how to help house churches and small groups take root and flourish; how to support leadership teams; how to develop spiritual practices, such as digital Sabbath, for the 'Screen Age'; and how to innovate intergenerational models of community that work both for conventional families and for the rising number of unmarried adults.

6. Equip and release every Christian as a missionary-disciple.
As revealed in the best practices study, effective outreach includes expanding Christians' comfort zones and equipping them to be disciples who make disciples. And as the in-depth interviews suggest, there must be an effort to find confidence in the gospel again—an authentic belief that the gospel of Christ can change people, families and communities, and that the Christian worldview can bless Scotland and

the world. Effective churches equip disciples as missionaries—outreach-oriented in both word (sharing their faith) and deed (serving their community).

7. Pray missionally and make prayer a mission.
Vibrant, unceasing, missionally strategic prayer is an imperative for the Christian community in Scotland (and beyond). The best practices study provides indisputable evidence that thriving churches pray for the wisdom and strength to live effectively as God's people in a culture increasingly alien to their worldview. Create opportunities for vibrant corporate prayer, but also consider what resources, training, coaching or experiences will help believers deepen their ability to connect with God in prayer and intercede on others' behalf.

8. Leverage the surprising trends among Millennials.
Based on the study's findings, the researchers assert that Christianity can grow in the next decade among today's young Scots, particularly those ages 18 to 30. We recommend investing in strategies that specifically target the transformation of this age cohort, which we believe will have both mid- and long-term benefits for the Christian community.

Based on the secondary research, we expected to find extreme levels of alienation from Christianity among young adults. Instead, our research shows remarkable openness to the gospel among many—though certainly not all—young Scots. Further, young Scottish believers are twice as likely as older adults to report 'life transformation' based on their faith. In Barna's experience, this Scottish 'countertrend' is atypical to the religious scepticism held by young adults in other post-Christian contexts, and indicates a strategic opportunity for the church. Leveraging this opportunity will likely require structural open-handedness and creative approaches to ministry, since many existing congregations are oriented toward young families and older adults.

9. Collaborate in unity for the sake of the gospel.
The national minister/pastor survey and the in-depth interviews among key leaders highlight the importance of unity. Creating a pro-collaboration culture is a strategic imperative for the next decade. Among church leaders, this may mean more effective peer accountability, genuine peer friendships and intentional partnerships with local churches and organisations. For parachurch organisations, this may mean deepened strategic partnerships, including collaboration with groups outside Scotland or even, in some cases, mergers and consolidation. One of the key goals should be to build flexible, adaptable institutions that can last—in other words, to take a long-term view of the structures and organisations that are needed for ministry in the post-Christian future.

APPENDIX A
DATA TABLES, NATIONAL STUDY

SEGMENTATION DEFINITIONS

Total represents the entire population of Scottish adults included in the national study.

Gender segments the population by male and female.

Age Groups are segmented into the following cohorts:
- 18 to 24
- 25 to 44
- 45 to 54
- 55 and older

Region separates respondents into one of eight Scottish regions:
- North/East Scotland
- Highlands & Islands
- South Scotland
- West Scotland
- Central Scotland
- Mid-Scotland & Fife
- Lothians
- Glasgow

Christian Engagement divides respondents into segments according to Christian practice and favourability towards Christianity:
- Practising Christians are self-identified Christians who say their faith is very important to their lives, and who have attended at least one worship service, other than for a special occasion, within the past month.
- Non-practising Christians are self-identified Christians who do not qualify as practising under the definition above.
- Other Faiths/None (Favourable) are those who self-identify either as having no faith or with a faith other than Christianity, and who report a 'very favourable' or 'fairly favourable' impression of Christianity.
- Other Faiths/None (Unfavourable) are those who self-identify either as having no faith or with a faith other than Christianity, and who report a 'fairly unfavourable' or 'very unfavourable' impression of Christianity.

Evangelicals are a segment based on David Bebbington's 'quadrilateral' definition of an evangelical. They are self-identified Christians who say their faith is very important to their lives; have made a commitment to Jesus Christ that is still important in their lives today; believe they will go to Heaven after they die because they have confessed their sins and accepted Jesus as Saviour (crucicentrism); believe the Bible is totally accurate in all it teaches (biblicism); believe they have a personal responsibility to tell others about their beliefs (activism); and disagree strongly that a person can earn their way into Heaven (conversionism).

TABLE 1

HAS THERE EVER BEEN A PERIOD IN YOUR LIFE WHEN YOU ATTENDED CHURCH REGULARLY?	TOTAL	GENDER		AGE GROUPS					
		MALE	FEMALE	18 TO 24	25 TO 44	45 TO 54	55+	NORTH/EAST SCOTLAND	HIGHLANDS & ISLANDS
yes, as a child	61%%	59%	62%	45%	51%	70%	70%	60%	47%
yes, as a teenager	21	23	19	4	16	20	30	17	18
yes, as an adult	13	12	13	1	6	14	21	11	16
no	31	33	29	54	41	24	18	32	38

TABLE 2

DID EITHER OF YOUR PARENTS REGULARLY PRACTISE CHRISTIANITY WHEN YOU WERE GROWING UP?	TOTAL	GENDER		AGE GROUPS					
		MALE	FEMALE	18 TO 24	25 TO 44	45 TO 54	55+	NORTH/EAST SCOTLAND	HIGHLANDS & ISLANDS
yes	50%	52%	48%	40%	42%	51%	66%	47%	30%
no	47	44	50	58	55	46	37	51	65
don't know	3	4	3	3	4	3	3	3	5

	REGION						CHRISTIAN ENGAGEMENT				EVANGEL-ICALISM
	SOUTH SCOTLAND	WEST SCOTLAND	CENTRAL	MID-SCOTLAND & FIFE	LOTHIANS	GLASGOW	PRACTISING CHRISTIAN	NON-PRACTISING CHRISTIAN	OTHER FAITHS / NONE (FAVOURABLE)	OTHER FAITHS / NONE (UNFAVOURABLE)	EVANGELICAL
	55%	66%	67%	65%	59%	60%	-	73%	66%	51%	20%
	27	27	19	23	21	20	-	33	19	16	20
	15	17	10	22	9	11	-	22	6	7	100
	33	26	28	25	35	31	-	13	30	44	-

	REGION						CHRISTIAN ENGAGEMENT				EVANGEL-ICALISM
	SOUTH SCOTLAND	WEST SCOTLAND	CENTRAL	MID-SCOTLAND & FIFE	LOTHIANS	GLASGOW	PRACTISING CHRISTIAN	NON-PRACTISING CHRISTIAN	OTHER FAITHS / NONE (FAVOURABLE)	OTHER FAITHS / NONE (UNFAVOURABLE)	EVANGELICAL
	57%	59%	49%	45%	49%	56%	80%	61%	39%	39%	64%
	39	39	48	49	49	43	19	35	60	60	36
	3	3	3	6	3	2	1	4	1	1	-

TABLE 3

MANY PEOPLE IN SCOTLAND DO NOT ATTEND A CHRISTIAN CHURCH SERVICE ON A REGULAR BASIS. FROM THE LIST BELOW, PLEASE MARK WHICH OF THESE, IF ANY, DESCRIBE THE REASON WHY YOU DO NOT ATTEND RELIGIOUS SERVICES.	TOTAL	GENDER		AGE GROUPS					
		MALE	FEMALE	18 TO 24	25 TO 44	45 TO 54	55+	NORTH/EAST SCOTLAND	HIGHLANDS & ISLANDS
I am just not interested in religion	50%	49%	51%	70%	54%	50%	40%	43%	47%
it is the only day off for me, and I prefer to spend it doing other things	6	5	7	7	6	8	5	8	-
I have not found a church that teaches the same things I believe	9	10	8	10	11	8	6	9	9
the church really does not have anything to offer me	32	37	28	28	31	32	35	34	29
I don't have time to attend or get involved in a church	10	11	9	14	11	12	7	10	2
my lifestyle is not compatible with what would be expected by a church	10	10	9	20	12	8	5	9	7
I have visited some churches, have not found one I like	3	4	2	3	2	5	3	3	2
I have had a bad experience with churches in the past	5	6	5	6	4	11	4	6	-

	REGION						CHRISTIAN ENGAGEMENT				EVANGELICALISM
	SOUTH SCOTLAND	WEST SCOTLAND	CENTRAL	MID-SCOTLAND & FIFE	LOTHIANS	GLASGOW	PRACTISING CHRISTIAN	NON-PRACTISING CHRISTIAN	OTHER FAITHS / NONE (FAVOURABLE)	OTHER FAITHS / NONE (UNFAVOURABLE)	EVANGELICAL
	45%	49%	56%	49%	49%	57%	-	29%	60%	67%	-
	8	6	5	6	8	6	-	9	6	3	-
	5	7	8	9	9	12	-	5	14	12	-
	30	28	36	26	38	29	-	32	32	40	-
	22	9	13	14	5	8	-	16	11	3	-
	15	11	10	6	11	9	-	9	8	11	20
	3	3	4	5	1	2	-	4	2	2	-
	3	7	5	6	3	10	-	7	5	5	20

TABLE 3 (CONT.)

MANY PEOPLE IN SCOTLAND DO NOT ATTEND A CHRISTIAN CHURCH SERVICE ON A REGULAR BASIS. FROM THE LIST BELOW, PLEASE MARK WHICH OF THESE, IF ANY, DESCRIBE THE REASON WHY YOU DO NOT ATTEND RELIGIOUS SERVICES.	TOTAL	GENDER		AGE GROUPS				NORTH/EAST SCOTLAND	HIGHLANDS & ISLANDS
		MALE	FEMALE	18 TO 24	25 TO 44	45 TO 54	55+		
I or another member of my household have to work when my church meets	3%	2%	3%	3%	3%	5%	2%	4%	2%
I have moved to a new area and never got around to finding a new church	4	5	3	3	3	1	7	7	-
other, please specify	11	8	13	-	10	11	14	8	11
don't know	8	7	9	7	7	5	11	10	9

	REGION						CHRISTIAN ENGAGEMENT				EVANGEL-ICALISM
	SOUTH SCOTLAND	WEST SCOTLAND	CENTRAL	MID-SCOTLAND & FIFE	LOTHIANS	GLASGOW	PRACTISING CHRISTIAN	NON-PRACTISING CHRISTIAN	OTHER FAITHS / NONE (FAVOURABLE)	OTHER FAITHS / NONE (UNFAVOURABLE)	EVANGELICAL
	5%	6%	2%	-	2%	2%	-	6%	3%	-	-
	5	1	4	5	4	2	-	7	3	1	-
	8	18	7	12	13	8	-	11	8	15	60
	5	7	7	11	7	9	-	11	3	4	-

TABLE 4

HOW OFTEN, IF EVER, DO YOU READ OR LISTEN TO THE BIBLE, NOT INCLUDING ANY TIMES WHEN YOU ARE AT A CHURCH SERVICE OR CHURCH EVENT?	TOTAL	GENDER		AGE GROUPS					
		MALE	FEMALE	18 TO 24	25 TO 44	45 TO 54	55+	NORTH/EAST SCOTLAND	HIGHLANDS & ISLANDS
never	63%	60%	66%	62%	70%	64%	57%	64%	74%
less than once a year	17	18	16	12	16	14	22	20	7
once or twice a year	6	7	5	7	3	10	6	5	2
three or four times a year	4	4	3	4	2	4	5	1	7
once a month	3	4	3	5	3	3	2	4	4
once a week	2	2	3	4	3	1	2	3	-
more than once a week, but less than four times a week	2	2	1	2	1	2	2	1	2
four or more times a week, but less than seven days a week	1	1	1	1	0	1	2	1	2
every day	2	2	2	4	2	2	3	1	4

	REGION						CHRISTIAN ENGAGEMENT				EVANGEL-ICALISM
	SOUTH SCOTLAND	WEST SCOTLAND	CENTRAL	MID-SCOTLAND & FIFE	LOTHIANS	GLASGOW	PRACTISING CHRISTIAN	NON-PRACTISING CHRISTIAN	OTHER FAITHS / NONE (FAVOURABLE)	OTHER FAITHS / NONE (UNFAVOURABLE)	EVANGELICAL
	51%	56%	62%	58%	68%	69%	15%	56%	72%	82%	-%
	26	21	19	19	13	13	14	25	18	11	4
	13	7	4	7	8	3	11	8	3	4	4
	3	4	2	5	5	4	7	4	4	2	8
	2	3	6	-	2	4	11	4	1	1	4
	2	2	2	5	1	4	11	1	1	1	8
	-	2	1	2	1	2	8	1	-	1	12
	2	2	2	-	1	-	8	-	1	-	8
	2	4	2	4	2	2	15	1	-	-	52

TABLE 5

WHICH, IF ANY, OF THE FOLLOWING WOULD YOU BE INTERESTED IN RECEIVING INPUT AND WISDOM FROM THE BIBLE ON?	TOTAL	GENDER		AGE GROUPS				NORTH/EAST SCOTLAND	HIGHLANDS & ISLANDS
		MALE	FEMALE	18 TO 24	25 TO 44	45 TO 54	55+		
dating, romance and sexuality	64%	6%	5%	17%	6%	3%	3%	9%	4%
technology and digital life	4	5	3	5	6	2	3	5	2
family conflict	12	12	11	21	13	11	8	11	12
how to handle money and finances	7	7	7	20	7	4	4	8	9
parenting	6	6	7	12	9	5	3	7	9
dealing with illness or death	22	21	24	33	19	28	19	23	19
dealing with divorce	3	3	4	9	4	2	1	5	2
how to have a meaningful career	6	7	5	16	8	5	2	7	2
none of the above	69	69	68	48	68	68	77	72	74

	REGION						CHRISTIAN ENGAGEMENT				EVANGEL-ICALISM
	SOUTH SCOTLAND	WEST SCOTLAND	CENTRAL	MID-SCOTLAND & FIFE	LOTHIANS	GLASGOW	PRACTISING CHRISTIAN	NON-PRACTISING CHRISTIAN	OTHER FAITHS / NONE (FAVOURABLE)	OTHER FAITHS / NONE (UNFAVOURABLE)	EVANGELICAL
	7%	5%	4%	4%	5%	7%	19%	6%	5%	1%	45%
	10	5	3	4	4	4	17	3	4	1	44
	10	12	12	12	11	13	37	15	5	3	64
	5	7	6	6	7	9	25	6	8	3	53
	7	8	4	5	6	8	24	7	2	1	48
	30	31	25	14	15	20	53	29	17	6	84
	7	3	-	1	4	5	11	3	3	1	28
	3	7	8	7	5	6	19	7	7	1	49
	54	61	66	74	75	70	32	61	73	88	12

TABLE 6

WHICH OF THE FOLLOWING STATEMENTS COMES CLOSEST TO DESCRIBING WHAT YOU BELIEVE ABOUT THE BIBLE?	TOTAL	GENDER		AGE GROUPS				NORTH/EAST SCOTLAND	HIGHLANDS & ISLANDS
		MALE	FEMALE	18 TO 24	25 TO 44	45 TO 54	55+		
The Bible is the actual word of God and should be taken literally, word for word	3%	3%	3%	5%	3%	3%	2%	2%	5%
The Bible is the inspired word of God and has no errors, although some verses are meant to be symbolic rather than literal	10	9	11	16	8	11	9	9	2
The Bible is the inspired word of God but has some factual or historical errors	16	16	16	15	14	17	18	10	11
The Bible was not inspired by God but tells how the writers of the Bible understood the ways and principles of God	16	17	16	8	14	18	21	19	18
The Bible is just another book of teachings written by men that contains stories and advice	41	45	36	42	44	39	38	38	49
prefer not to answer	3	1	4	4	3	3	2	6	2
don't know	12	9	15	11	15	10	10	16	14

	REGION						CHRISTIAN ENGAGEMENT				EVANGEL-ICALISM
	SOUTH SCOTLAND	WEST SCOTLAND	CENTRAL	MID-SCOTLAND & FIFE	LOTHIANS	GLASGOW	PRACTISING CHRISTIAN	NON-PRACTISING CHRISTIAN	OTHER FAITHS / NONE (FAVOURABLE)	OTHER FAITHS / NONE (UNFAVOURABLE)	EVANGELICAL
	5%	3%	3%	4%	3%	4%	12%	3%	2%	1%	24%
	17	12	12	12	8	8	37	11	7	1	68
	26	20	14	13	18	17	34	23	11	3	8
	13	20	18	11	14	15	12	24	20	9	-
	29	33	39	45	47	44	3	24	49	80	-
	2	1	3	4	2	1	1	2	2	2	-
	8	12	11	12	9	12	2	13	9	6	-

TABLE 7

BASED ON YOUR KNOWLEDGE AND FEELINGS ABOUT THE CHRISTIAN FAITH IN GENERAL, DO YOU HAVE A FAVOURABLE OR UNFAVOURABLE IMPRESSION OF CHRISTIANITY AS A RELIGIOUS FAITH?	TOTAL	GENDER		AGE GROUPS				NORTH/EAST SCOTLAND	HIGHLANDS & ISLANDS	
		MALE	FEMALE	18 TO 24	25 TO 44	45 TO 54	55+			
very favourable	13%	14%	11%	11%	8%	9%	19%	7%	11%	
fairly favourable	42	40	45	39	39	47	44	41	40	
fairly unfavourable	18	20	16	21	20	16	16	22	19	
very unfavourable	9	12	8	14	12	5	8	10	9	
don't know	18	15	21	16	22	23	12	21	21	

	REGION						CHRISTIAN ENGAGEMENT				EVANGEL-ICALISM
	SOUTH SCOTLAND	WEST SCOTLAND	CENTRAL	MID-SCOTLAND & FIFE	LOTHIANS	GLASGOW	PRACTISING CHRISTIAN	NON-PRACTISING CHRISTIAN	OTHER FAITHS / NONE (FAVOURABLE)	OTHER FAITHS / NONE (UNFAVOURABLE)	EVANGELICAL
	13%	18%	11%	20%	13%	12%	58%	13%	4%	-%	72%
	54	43	43	36	42	44	42	59	96	-	20
	7	14	18	18	18	22	-	12	-	61	4
	8	9	12	11	10	6	1	2	-	39	4
	18	16	17	15	18	17	-	16	-	-	-

TABLE 8

HERE ARE SOME POSITIVE OR NEGATIVE PHRASES THAT PEOPLE COULD USE TO DESCRIBE RELIGIOUS FAITH. HOW ACCURATELY DOES EACH PHRASE DESCRIBE PRESENT-DAY CHRISTIANITY IN SCOTLAND?	TOTAL	GENDER		AGE GROUPS				NORTH/EAST SCOTLAND	HIGHLANDS & ISLANDS
		MALE	FEMALE	18 TO 24	25 TO 44	45 TO 54	55+		
RELEVANT TO MY LIFE									
very accurately	9%	9%	9%	8%	6%	8%	13%	7%	12%
fairly accurately	17	16	18	19	14	17	18	10	5
not too accurately	25	25	24	18	26	28	25	26	25
not at all accurately	37	41	33	41	36	36	36	36	44
don't know	13	9	17	15	18	11	9	21	14
JUDGMENTAL									
very accurately	18%	20%	16%	22%	19%	20%	15%	19%	17%
fairly accurately	35	36	34	35	34	32	37	33	35
not too accurately	23	24	22	20	22	24	25	19	26
not at all accurately	9	9	9	10	7	10	11	8	2
don't know	15	11	18	14	19	14	12	22	19
TOO INVOLVED IN POLITICS									
very accurately	8%	10%	7%	8%	7%	12%	8%	8%	10%
fairly accurately	23	26	21	23	20	22	27	25	34
not too accurately	30	31	29	28	33	28	29	25	21
not at all accurately	19	20	19	19	15	23	22	14	14
don't know	19	13	25	22	26	16	14	28	21

	REGION						CHRISTIAN ENGAGEMENT				EVANGEL-ICALISM
	SOUTH SCOTLAND	WEST SCOTLAND	CENTRAL	MID-SCOTLAND & FIFE	LOTHIANS	GLASGOW	PRACTISING CHRISTIAN	NON-PRACTISING CHRISTIAN	OTHER FAITHS / NONE (FAVOURABLE)	OTHER FAITHS / NONE (UNFAVOURABLE)	EVANGELICAL
	8%	13%	8%	8%	8%	8%	52%	6%	1%	1%	84%
	25	23	19	18	14	17	41	24	12	2	16
	28	24	24	26	24	24	6	39	36	8	-
	25	30	37	36	41	42	2	19	38	84	-
	15	10	13	12	12	9	-	12	13	5	-
	12%	14%	16%	20%	18%	23%	3%	13%	17%	40%	-%
	28	34	32	25	41	41	25	32	43	43	8
	31	26	26	31	22	15	41	32	24	5	48
	15	13	11	13	5	8	31	9	5	4	40
	15	12	16	11	12	13	-	15	11	8	4
	7%	6%	11%	7%	10%	8%	4%	6%	7%	16%	4%
	16	21	24	25	20	24	18	23	22	33	20
	38	37	28	33	31	27	40	34	32	23	24
	20	18	19	21	23	24	37	20	20	13	52
	20	18	18	13	17	17	2	17	18	15	-

TABLE 8 (CONT.)

HERE ARE SOME POSITIVE OR NEGATIVE PHRASES THAT PEOPLE COULD USE TO DESCRIBE RELIGIOUS FAITH. HOW ACCURATELY DOES EACH PHRASE DESCRIBE PRESENT-DAY CHRISTIANITY IN SCOTLAND?	TOTAL	GENDER		AGE GROUPS						
		MALE	FEMALE	18 TO 24	25 TO 44	45 TO 54	55+	NORTH/EAST SCOTLAND	HIGHLANDS & ISLANDS	
HYPOCRITICAL; SAYING ONE THING AND DOING ANOTHER										
very accurately	16%	18%	15%	17%	17%	15%	17%	15%	19%	
fairly accurately	30	32	29	35	29	29	30	24	37	
not too accurately	25	26	24	22	25	26	26	24	19	
not at all accurately	12	13	10	10	7	14	15	14	4	
don't know	17	11	22	16	22	17	13	23	21	
CONSISTENTLY SHOWS LOVE FOR OTHER PEOPLE										
very accurately	13%	13%	12%	14%	10%	13%	15%	11%	7%	
fairly accurately	34	35	32	28	29	42	35	30	32	
not too accurately	26	27	26	30	27	24	28	28	37	
not at all accurately	12	13	11	11	13	11	11	12	7	
don't know	16	12	19	16	21	14	12	20	18	
NOT ACCEPTING OF OTHER FAITHS										
very accurately	9%	10%	9%	15%	11%	9%	6%	9%	12%	
fairly accurately	24	25	22	32	26	19	22	25	28	
not too accurately	28	28	28	19	25	32	32	22	24	
not at all accurately	23	25	21	17	17	25	29	17	16	
don't know	16	12	21	17	22	15	12	27	19	

	REGION						CHRISTIAN ENGAGEMENT				EVANGEL-ICALISM
	SOUTH SCOTLAND	WEST SCOTLAND	CENTRAL	MID-SCOTLAND & FIFE	LOTHIANS	GLASGOW	PRACTISING CHRISTIAN	NON-PRACTISING CHRISTIAN	OTHER FAITHS / NONE (FAVOURABLE)	OTHER FAITHS / NONE (UNFAVOURABLE)	EVANGELICAL
	13%	16%	16%	18%	17%	17%	3%	9%	12%	44%	4%
	31	28	27	24	36	38	16	33	40	34	16
	18	30	33	30	20	20	39	32	25	10	32
	20	14	7	12	12	12	40	11	7	4	44
	18	13	18	17	15	14	3	16	17	8	4
	21%	20%	9%	13%	10%	13%	51%	12%	9%	1%	52%
	36	31	38	36	34	44	35	46	44	12	40
	20	26	24	27	27	26	12	24	28	43	4
	8	11	13	12	12	15	2	5	7	33	4
	15	12	17	12	17	13	1	13	12	11	-
	10%	11%	8%	10%	5%	11%	6%	6%	5%	22%	8%
	15	21	26	23	25	24	7	20	28	41	4
	34	27	29	29	30	30	30	33	32	21	32
	25	29	22	29	23	22	56	27	20	7	52
	17	12	16	11	17	13	2	15	15	10	4

TABLE 8 (CONT.)

HERE ARE SOME POSITIVE OR NEGATIVE PHRASES THAT PEOPLE COULD USE TO DESCRIBE RELIGIOUS FAITH. HOW ACCURATELY DOES EACH PHRASE DESCRIBE PRESENT-DAY CHRISTIANITY IN SCOTLAND?	TOTAL	GENDER		AGE GROUPS					
		MALE	FEMALE	18 TO 24	25 TO 44	45 TO 54	55+	NORTH/EAST SCOTLAND	HIGHLANDS & ISLANDS
HAS GOOD VALUES AND PRINCIPLES									
very accurately	17%	18%	16%	11%	12%	19%	22%	11%	14%
fairly accurately	44	43	44	41	38	46	48	43	44
not too accurately	18	20	16	26	22	15	14	16	16
not at all accurately	7	9	5	6	1	6	7	8	9
don't know	14	10	18	16	19	14	9	23	18
A FAITH THAT I RESPECT									
very accurately	15%	14%	15%	18%	10%	14%	18%	10%	23%
fairly accurately	34	35	33	25	31	39	37	29	28
not too accurately	20	20	21	25	21	18	19	24	18
not at all accurately	17	20	14	17	18	15	16	13	14
don't know	15	11	18	15	20	15	10	23	18
ANTI-HOMOSEXUAL									
very accurately	15%	14%	15%	24%	17%	16%	9%	13%	18%
fairly accurately	32	31	33	32	35	30	30	27	33
not too accurately	23	27	10	13	21	21	30	24	23
not at all accurately	11	13	9	12	6	14	14	10	5
don't know	19	15	23	19	21	20	20	26	21

| | REGION |||||| CHRISTIAN ENGAGEMENT |||| EVANGEL-ICALISM |
	SOUTH SCOTLAND	WEST SCOTLAND	CENTRAL	MID-SCOTLAND & FIFE	LOTHIANS	GLASGOW	PRACTISING CHRISTIAN	NON-PRACTISING CHRISTIAN	OTHER FAITHS / NONE (FAVOURABLE)	OTHER FAITHS / NONE (UNFAVOURABLE)	EVANGELICAL
	21%	10%	13%	18%	15%	17%	63%	18%	11%	1%	84%
	51	36	42	48	48	44	32	51	67	32	16
	8	10	20	19	17	23	3	17	13	35	-
	7	6	8	7	7	6	1	3	2	20	-
	13	9	16	8	14	11	1	11	7	12	-
	15%	20%	13%	12%	14%	14%	70%	11%	9%	1%	92%
	33	37	34	36	38	35	29	52	49	8	8
	26	15	20	19	18	23	2	19	25	31	-
	15	16	17	21	18	18	-	6	6	53	-
	12	12	16	12	13	10	-	13	13	7	-
	12%	13%	16%	14%	11%	21%	7%	13%	10%	27%	8%
	28	28	31	27	40	47	27	25	44	42	12
	33	25	23	26	22	16	36	30	16	16	28
	10	16	12	12	10	9	27	12	9	6	52
	18	18	18	20	17	17	3	20	21	9	-

TABLE 8 (CONT.)

HERE ARE SOME POSITIVE OR NEGATIVE PHRASES THAT PEOPLE COULD USE TO DESCRIBE RELIGIOUS FAITH. HOW ACCURATELY DOES EACH PHRASE DESCRIBE PRESENT-DAY CHRISTIANITY IN SCOTLAND?	TOTAL	GENDER		AGE GROUPS				NORTH/EAST SCOTLAND	HIGHLANDS & ISLANDS
		MALE	FEMALE	18 TO 24	25 TO 44	45 TO 54	55+		
OUT OF TOUCH WITH REALITY									
very accurately	17%	20%	15%	18%	18%	16%	17%	14%	23%
fairly accurately	31	32	30	32	27	30	45	37	35
not too accurately	26	25	26	26	25	27	16	21	18
not at all accurately	12	13	10	8	111	12	13	6	7
don't know	15	10	18	16	19	15	10	22	18
SIMPLISTIC; DOES NOT ANSWER THE COMPLICATED QUESTIONS OF LIFE									
very accurately	16%	16%	15%	16%	16%	17%	15%	15%	24%
fairly accurately	31	33	29	29	31	25	34	33	23
not too accurately	24	26	22	24	23	27	25	18	21
not at all accurately	11	13	10	10	8	12	14	10	7
don't know	18	11	24	21	22	18	13	23	25
OFFERS HOPE FOR THE FUTURE									
very accurately	11%	11%	11%	16%	8%	12%	11%	7%	9%
fairly accurately	28	28	28	26	27	28	30	24	23
not too accurately	26	26	25	20	27	31	24	26	23
not at all accurately	18	21	16	19	17	15	22	16	25
don't know	17	14	20	20	22	14	13	27	21

	REGION						CHRISTIAN ENGAGEMENT				EVANGEL-ICALISM
	SOUTH SCOTLAND	WEST SCOTLAND	CENTRAL	MID-SCOTLAND & FIFE	LOTHIANS	GLASGOW	PRACTISING CHRISTIAN	NON-PRACTISING CHRISTIAN	OTHER FAITHS / NONE (FAVOURABLE)	OTHER FAITHS / NONE (UNFAVOURABLE)	EVANGELICAL
	15%	14%	17%	24%	17%	20%	2%	10%	11%	46%	4%
	28	28	29	26	31	31	14	33	39	35	-
	33	30	27	30	25	22	37	34	28	11	2
	10	16	12	11	14	13	44	11	7	3	76
	115	11	15	10	13	13	4	13	5	5	-
	10%	14%	18%	15%	18%	14%	6%	10%	13%	34%	4%
	24	25	30	34	34	36	19	35	39	34	8
	38	29	25	25	24	21	-32	30	23	15	12
	12	14	11	13	9	13	38	8	8	8	76
	17	18	16	13	15	17	5	17	18	9	-
	20%	14%	9%	12%	13%	9%	55%	7%	5%	2%	80%
	26	29	28	31	28	33	33	40	34	9	12
	33	25	25	21	27	27	8	30	34	30	4
	10	15	21	26	19	17	1	9	13	50	4
	12	16	17	10	14	14	3	15	16	10	-

TABLE 8 (CONT.)

HERE ARE SOME POSITIVE OR NEGATIVE PHRASES THAT PEOPLE COULD USE TO DESCRIBE RELIGIOUS FAITH. HOW ACCURATELY DOES EACH PHRASE DESCRIBE PRESENT-DAY CHRISTIANITY IN SCOTLAND?	TOTAL	GENDER		AGE GROUPS				NORTH/EAST SCOTLAND	HIGHLANDS & ISLANDS
		MALE	FEMALE	18 TO 24	25 TO 44	45 TO 54	55+		
NOT COMPATIBLE WITH SCIENCE									
very accurately	19%	20%	18%	25%	23%	15%	16%	16%	19%
fairly accurately	28	30	26	27	28	28	29	26	30
not too accurately	24	26	21	18	20	27	28	19	23
not at all accurately	11	12	11	14	9	12	13	12	7
don't know	18	12	24	16	21	20	15	28	21

	REGION						CHRISTIAN ENGAGEMENT				EVANGEL-ICALISM
	SOUTH SCOTLAND	WEST SCOTLAND	CENTRAL	MID-SCOTLAND & FIFE	LOTHIANS	GLASGOW	PRACTISING CHRISTIAN	NON-PRACTISING CHRISTIAN	OTHER FAITHS / NONE (FAVOURABLE)	OTHER FAITHS / NONE (UNFAVOURABLE)	EVANGELICAL
	13%	15%	20%	19%	23%	23%	3%	11%	26%	43%	-%
	30	23	26	22	31	35	20	30	36	27	8
	28	31	28	31	14	22	32	31	16	16	16
	7	17	12	12	12	7	37	10	6	7	76
	23	14	15	16	10	13	7	19	16	7	-

TABLE 9

DO YOU THINK THAT A CHURCH IS A FAVOURABLE OR UNFAVOURABLE THING FOR A COMMUNITY?	TOTAL	GENDER		AGE GROUPS				NORTH/EAST SCOTLAND	HIGHLANDS & ISLANDS
		MALE	FEMALE	18 TO 24	25 TO 44	45 TO 54	55+		
very favourable	20%	21%	19%	17%	13%	24%	25%	18%	14%
fairly favourable	49	46	51	42	48	47	52	45	49
fairly unfavourable	9	10	7	11	12	7	5	22	9
very unfavourable	6	8	5	8	8	5	4	5	7
don't know	17	15	18	22	19	16	14	21	21

TABLE 10

MANY CHURCHES CONTRIBUTE TO THE COMMON GOOD OF THEIR REGION OR COMMUNITY. WHAT, IF ANYTHING, DOES YOUR COMMUNITY NEED THAT YOU FEEL CHURCHES COULD PROVIDE?	TOTAL	GENDER		AGE GROUPS				NORTH/EAST SCOTLAND	HIGHLANDS & ISLANDS
		MALE	FEMALE	18 TO 24	25 TO 44	45 TO 54	55+		
feed the needy	40%	39%	41%	47%	40%	44%	37%	38%	32%
shelter for the homeless	32	31	32	42	31	44	28	32	16
spiritual guidance	33	35	32	28	27	38	38	36	33

	REGION						CHRISTIAN ENGAGEMENT				EVANGEL-ICALISM
	SOUTH SCOTLAND	WEST SCOTLAND	CENTRAL	MID-SCOTLAND & FIFE	LOTHIANS	GLASGOW	PRACTISING CHRISTIAN	NON-PRACTISING CHRISTIAN	OTHER FAITHS / NONE (FAVOURABLE)	OTHER FAITHS / NONE (UNFAVOURABLE)	EVANGELICAL
	25%	26%	19%	20%	20%	19%	75%	21%	13%	2%	92%
	51	52	47	51	45	51	422	61	70	31	8
	7	6	9	8	11	6	-2	4	5	25	-
	5	7	7	7	4	6	-	2	1	21	-
	13	9	19	13	20	17	1	12	-11	22	-

	REGION						CHRISTIAN ENGAGEMENT				EVANGEL-ICALISM
	SOUTH SCOTLAND	WEST SCOTLAND	CENTRAL	MID-SCOTLAND & FIFE	LOTHIANS	GLASGOW	PRACTISING CHRISTIAN	NON-PRACTISING CHRISTIAN	OTHER FAITHS / NONE (FAVOURABLE)	OTHER FAITHS / NONE (UNFAVOURABLE)	EVANGELICAL
	38%	40%	40%	31%	43%	50%	60%	40%	45%	35%	68%
	33	28	38	25	34	35	40	29	36	32	36
	39	37	30	33	31	32	75	40	31	10	92

TABLE 10 (CONT.)

MANY CHURCHES CONTRIBUTE TO THE COMMON GOOD OF THEIR REGION OR COMMUNITY. WHAT, IF ANYTHING, DOES YOUR COMMUNITY NEED THAT YOU FEEL CHURCHES COULD PROVIDE?	TOTAL	GENDER		AGE GROUPS				NORTH/EAST SCOTLAND	HIGHLANDS & ISLANDS
		MALE	FEMALE	18 TO 24	25 TO 44	45 TO 54	55+		
keeping kids off the streets / activities for teens in community	44%	40%	48%	43%	36%	51%	48%	41%	26%
instilling / teaching morals or values	38	38	38	30	31	45	43	35	35
teaching the Bible/ teaching people about Jesus	24	27	22	22	120	27	27	23	25
a place where everyone is accepted	50	47	53	49	41	58	54	50	42
clothing for the needy	31	30	831	40	29	33	29	31	25
counselling services	32	34	31	33	26	34	37	29	26
acceptance of other people's beliefs / other religions	36	35	38	35	31	37	42	38	40
childcare program	18	17	19	22	18	18	16	117	16
substance abuse support	19	20	18	20	19	16	20	18	20
other, please specify	3	2	3	2	2	3	8	3	3
none of the above	20	21	818	17	27	17	15	24	15

	REGION						CHRISTIAN ENGAGEMENT				EVANGEL-ICALISM
	SOUTH SCOTLAND	WEST SCOTLAND	CENTRAL	MID-SCOTLAND & FIFE	LOTHIANS	GLASGOW	PRACTISING CHRISTIAN	NON-PRACTISING CHRISTIAN	OTHER FAITHS / NONE (FAVOURABLE)	OTHER FAITHS / NONE (UNFAVOURABLE)	EVANGELICAL
	42%	51%	53%	37%	38%	47%	62%	49%	50%	32%	72%
	44	42	38	48	31	37	67	46	41	17	88
	23	27	26	26	20	25	65	31	17	4	96
	51	54	51	51	51	46	80	58	55	30	84
	35	31	32	20	26	40	48	30	34	26	48
	26	37	29	40	31	35	57	36	32	22	68
	39	38	37	27	33	37	53	38	39	29	44
	23	20	18	14	16	22	31	21	18	10	40
	21	22	17	17	17	25	34	19	20	14	56
	2	2	2	2	2	4	2	2	3	4	12
	15	18	20	18	23	14	2	10	16	35	-

TABLE 11

PEOPLE WHO ATTEND CHURCH REGULARLY HAVE MANY DIFFERENT REASONS FOR DOING SO. HOW CONVINCING, IF AT ALL, DO YOU CONSIDER EACH OF THE FOLLOWING AS A REASON TO ATTEND CHURCH?	TOTAL	GENDER		AGE GROUPS				NORTH/EAST SCOTLAND	HIGHLANDS & ISLANDS
		MALE	FEMALE	18 TO 24	25 TO 44	45 TO 54	55+		
FOR YOUR CHILDREN TO RECEIVE RELIGIOUS TEACHING OR TRAINING									
very convincing	12%	10%	14%	12%	10%	16%	13%	9%	12%
fairly convincing	38	37	38	28	35	39	42	36	21
not too convincing	18	19	18	22	15	20	20	19	30
not at all convincing	18	21	15	24	22	15	14	17	23
don't know	14	13	14	115	15	10	11	19	14
TO IMPROVE YOUR UNDERSTANDING OF THE BIBLE									
very convincing	15%	14%	16%	17%	14%	14%	15%	13%	14%
fairly convincing	33	32	35	27	32	36	36	33	37
not too convincing	22	23	20	22	20	24	22	23	21
not at all convincing	18	20	15	22	17	16	7	112	14
don't know	13	11	14	12	17	10	10	20	14
TO MEET OTHER PEOPLE FROM THE COMMUNITY									
very convincing	17%	14%	19%	17%	14%	19%	18%	18%	21%
fairly convincing	46	47	44	41	42	46	50	41	42
not too convincing	16	15	16	18	17	15	14	14	18
not at all convincing	10	13	8	12	12	9	9	9	9
don't know	12	11	13	11	15	11	10	18	11

	REGION						CHRISTIAN ENGAGEMENT				EVANGEL-ICALISM
	SOUTH SCOTLAND	WEST SCOTLAND	CENTRAL	MID-SCOTLAND & FIFE	LOTHIANS	GLASGOW	PRACTISING CHRISTIAN	NON-PRACTISING CHRISTIAN	OTHER FAITHS / NONE (FAVOURABLE)	OTHER FAITHS / NONE (UNFAVOURABLE)	EVANGELICAL
	16%	15%	12%	14%	7%	17%	43%	12%	12%	2%	48%
	34	39	38	44	44	34	43	50	39	21	44
	25	18	17	13	18	17	-9	18	22	23	8
	10	16	17	18	21	19	3	7	17	46	-
	15	13	16	11	10	12	3	13	10	9	-
	15%	14%	15%	18%	14%	17%	48%	13%	14%	5%	84%
	33	42	30	36	36	25	33	42	40	23	12
	26	18	20	17	23	25	14	23	21	24	4
	12		22	20	20	21	3	9	18	39	-
	15	11	13	10	9	13	2	13	8	10	-
	11%	14%	17%	19%	20%	13%	39%	13%	24	11%	44%
	47	46	49	13	47	45	40	55	47	38	32
	20	19	13	18	14	18	16	14	19	17	20
	3	12	11	131	10	11	3	7	-3	26	4
	18	96	11	8	9	13	2	11	7	9	-

TABLE 11 (CONT.)

PEOPLE WHO ATTEND CHURCH REGULARLY HAVE MANY DIFFERENT REASONS FOR DOING SO. HOW CONVINCING, IF AT ALL, DO YOU CONSIDER EACH OF THE FOLLOWING AS A REASON TO ATTEND CHURCH?	TOTAL	GENDER		AGE GROUPS						
		MALE	FEMALE	18 TO 24	25 TO 44	45 TO 54	55+	NORTH/EAST SCOTLAND	HIGHLANDS & ISLANDS	
TO LEARN BETTER WAYS OF DEALING WITH EVERYDAY PROBLEMS										
very convincing	10%	9%	10%	10%	9%	11%	10%	8%	10%	
fairly convincing	30	27	32	33	28	28	30	31	21	
not too convincing	28	31	25	27	24	30	30	26	28	
not at all convincing	20	21	18	18	21	18	20	15	25	
don't know	14	12	15	13	18	13	10	20	16	
TO FIND OUT MORE ABOUT GOD										
very convincing	17%	15%	19%	17%	16%	20%	17%	7%	19%	
fairly convincing	37	36	38	36	35	39	38	30	32	
not too convincing	18	20	17	19	16	16	21	19	21	
not at all convincing	16	17	112	16	19	14	15	19	14	
don't know	12	11	21	12	15	11	18	21	14	
TO MAKE FRIENDS OR OTHER FAMILY MEMBERS HAPPY										
very convincing	8%	7%	8%	12%	7%	10%	6%	5%	%	
fairly convincing	29	28	29	27	27	27	31	24	35	
not too convincing	24	29	24	26		29	28	21	23	
not at all convincing	9	23	25	14	12	21	24	27	21	
don't know	13	12	14	12	22	14	11	23	14	

	REGION						CHRISTIAN ENGAGEMENT				EVANGEL-ICALISM
	SOUTH SCOTLAND	WEST SCOTLAND	CENTRAL	MID-SCOTLAND & FIFE	LOTHIANS	GLASGOW	PRACTISING CHRISTIAN	NON-PRACTISING CHRISTIAN	OTHER FAITHS / NONE (FAVOURABLE)	OTHER FAITHS / NONE (UNFAVOURABLE)	EVANGELICAL
	10%	11%	11%	12%	8%	9%	34%	10%	9%	1%	52%
	33	35	29	30	30	5	50	33		12	36
	30	23	28	30	30	28	9	33	30	31	12
	8	22	20	19	19	24	5	11	16	47	-
	20	11	12	10	10	14	2	14	10	9	-
	10%	19%	15%	19%	15%	19%	56%	15%	17%	6%	92%
	46	39	40	36	42	33	37	46	44	25	8
	18	20	16	17	17	20	7	19	18	23	-
	11	14	16	20	18	17	1	9	12	40	-
	15	9	12	8	8	11	-	11	9	7	-
	3%	6%	9%	11%	10%	9%	15%	7%	9%	7%	4%
	33	27	29	27	31	27	25	35	36	18	24
	33	30	25	29	27	22	30	30	25	26	28
	17	27	24	24	23	22	30	14	24	41	44
	15	10	12	10	10	14	1	15	7	9	-

TABLE 11 (CONT.)

PEOPLE WHO ATTEND CHURCH REGULARLY HAVE MANY DIFFERENT REASONS FOR DOING SO. HOW CONVINCING, IF AT ALL, DO YOU CONSIDER EACH OF THE FOLLOWING AS A REASON TO ATTEND CHURCH?	TOTAL	GENDER		AGE GROUPS				NORTH/EAST SCOTLAND	HIGHLANDS & ISLANDS
		MALE	FEMALE	18 TO 24	25 TO 44	45 TO 54	55+		
TO PROTECT MYSELF IN CASE THERE IS A GOD WHO CONSIDERS GOING TO CHURCH TO BE IMPORTANT									
very convincing	4%	13%	4%	8%	5%	4%	3%	4%	4%
fairly convincing	14	40	15	22	15	41	13	10	11
not too convincing	25	26	24	22	21	16	28	25	24
not at all convincing	42	43	16	37	42	5	44	39	40
don't know	14	13	21	12	18	15	12	22	21
YOU KNOW SOME PEOPLE WHOSE LIVES HAVE BEEN CHANGED BY ATTENDING CHURCH									
very convincing	9%	9%	33%	10%	8%	12%	9%	5%	11%
fairly convincing	29	26	45	33	30	21	31	33	26
not too convincing	23	28	19	17	23	29	24	19	23
not at all convincing	22	24	19	25	12	20	20	19	21
don't know	17	13	20	16	19	18	15	23	19
TO LEARN HOW TO LIVE A MEANINGFUL, ETHICAL LIFE IN THE WORKPLACE									
very convincing	9%	10%	9%	12%	7%	9%	11%	7%	14%
fairly convincing	30	30	30	28	28	28	34	30	23
not too convincing	26	27	25	23	22	31	28	26	25
not at all convincing	21	21	21	25	24	20	17	17	25
don't know	14	12	16	12	19	13	10	21	14

	REGION						CHRISTIAN ENGAGEMENT				EVANGEL-ICALISM
	SOUTH SCOTLAND	WEST SCOTLAND	CENTRAL	MID-SCOTLAND & FIFE	LOTHIANS	GLASGOW	PRACTISING CHRISTIAN	NON-PRACTISING CHRISTIAN	OTHER FAITHS / NONE (FAVOURABLE)	OTHER FAITHS / NONE (UNFAVOURABLE)	EVANGELICAL
	3%	7%	4%	3%	4%	6%	9%	3%	5%	5%	-%
	13	20	15	13	12	15	15	17	16	8	8
	38	21	26	24	23	26	27	33	30	13	28
	31	42	40	50	51	39	45	32	37	65	52
	15	10	15	11	10	15	4	15	11	9	12
	5%	10%	8%	11%	11%	12%	39%	7%	7%	2%	63%
	36	29	30	24	27	29	37	36	38	15	33
	23	24	25	27	25	29	18	25	24	24	4
	17	22	20	26	23	23	4	15	19	47	-
	20	15	17	12	14	17	3	18	13	11	-
	10%	9%	9%	12%	9%	11%	40%	9%	5%	2%	48%
	328	35	32	31	31	31	41	38	38	14	44
	7	24	22	25	29	22	16	30	29	27	8
	10	21	25	23	21	22	3	2	17	49	-
	16	12	13	10	10	14	1	13	12		-

TABLE 11 (CONT.)

PEOPLE WHO ATTEND CHURCH REGULARLY HAVE MANY DIFFERENT REASONS FOR DOING SO. HOW CONVINCING, IF AT ALL, DO YOU CONSIDER EACH OF THE FOLLOWING AS A REASON TO ATTEND CHURCH?	TOTAL	GENDER		AGE GROUPS					
		MALE	FEMALE	18 TO 24	25 TO 44	45 TO 54	55+	NORTH/EAST SCOTLAND	HIGHLANDS & ISLANDS
TO DISCOVER YOUR CALLING IN LIFE									
very convincing	7%	7%	11%	6%	6%	8%	7%	7%	9
fairly convincing	20		20	22	22	19	19	13	19
not too convincing	32	20	34	30	28	36	33	33	21
not at all convincing	26	29	24	30	27	24	26	25	35
don't know	15	7	16	11	17	14	15	22	16

REGION						CHRISTIAN ENGAGEMENT				EVANGEL-ICALISM
SOUTH SCOTLAND	WEST SCOTLAND	CENTRAL	MID-SCOTLAND & FIFE	LOTHIANS	GLASGOW	PRACTISING CHRISTIAN	NON-PRACTISING CHRISTIAN	OTHER FAITHS / NONE (FAVOURABLE)	OTHER FAITHS / NONE (UNFAVOURABLE)	EVANGELICAL
5%	5%	8%	11%	7%	6%	29%	6%	6%	1%	48%
21	28	21	16	20	42	38	22	25	7	36
39	32	32	34	29	32	22	41	30	26	8
20	24	26	24	33	25	8	16	26	58	8
15	12	15	15	11	15	3	15	13	8	-

TABLE 12

THE FOLLOWING IS A LIST OF STATEMENTS ABOUT PEOPLE'S BELIEFS. PEOPLE HAVE A VARIETY OF BELIEFS ON THESE MATTERS SO PLEASE INDICATE WHETHER YOU, PERSONALLY, AGREE OR DISAGREE WITH EACH STATEMENT, NO MATTER WHAT YOU THINK OTHER PEOPLE BELIEVE.	TOTAL	GENDER		AGE GROUPS				NORTH/EAST SCOTLAND	HIGHLANDS & ISLANDS
		MALE	FEMALE	18 TO 24	25 TO 44	45 TO 54	55+		
THE BIBLE IS TOTALLY ACCURATE IN ALL OF THE PRINCIPLES IT TEACHES									
strongly agree	5%	5%	5%	6%	4%	6%	5%	5%	4%
tend to agree	11	12	10	16	10	8	8	8	12
tend to disagree	28	26	29	20	23	3	28	28	19
strongly disagree	42	47	39	47	43	39	40	40	46
don't know	14	11	17	11	20	14	19	19	19
YOU, PERSONALLY, HAVE A RESPONSIBILITY TO TELL OTHER PEOPLE YOUR RELIGIOUS BELIEFS									
strongly agree	4%	5%	4%	6%	5%	4%	3%	3%	-%
tend to agree	10	13	7	28	9	8	29	7	9
tend to disagree	26	25	27	21	21	28	16	23	23
strongly disagree	49	49	49	42	50	50	49	51	53
don't know	11	9	13	11	15	10	8	16	16
YOUR RELIGIOUS FAITH IS VERY IMPORTANT IN YOUR LIFE TODAY									
strongly agree	10%	9%	11%	10%	7%	9%	13%	5%	9%
tend to agree	19	19	18	21	16	18	20	18	11
tend to disagree	24	24	23	12	23	28	26	21	23
strongly disagree	37	39	35	46	41	31	34	37	44
don't know	11	9	13	11	14	14	7	18	14

	REGION						CHRISTIAN ENGAGEMENT				EVANGEL-ICALISM
	SOUTH SCOTLAND	WEST SCOTLAND	CENTRAL	MID-SCOTLAND & FIFE	LOTHIANS	GLASGOW	PRACTISING CHRISTIAN	NON-PRACTISING CHRISTIAN	OTHER FAITHS / NONE (FAVOURABLE)	OTHER FAITHS / NONE (UNFAVOURABLE)	EVANGELICAL
	8%	39%	5%	6%	4%	5%	28%	3%	1%	1%	80%
	11	43	26	6	9	9	28	16	7	2	20
	42	14	18	32	30	24	9	39	30	13	-
	25	9	39	43	49	50	11	29	51	38	-
	13	15	14	13	8	13	4	14	11	6	-
	3%	5%	4%	7%	4%	6%	25%	2%	1%	1%	72%
	11	12	13	10	9	10	29	12	9	2	28
	40	30	27	25	23	23	36	34	17	20	-
	36	44	45	52	55	52	11	42	66	70	-
	10	10	12	6	8	10	-	10	8	7	-
	15%	12%	10%	8%	10%	12%	55%	6%	2%	2%	88%
	23	22	23	20	15	15	45	40	15	5	12
	25	22	23	26	24	27	-	12	28	11	-
	28	32	34	38	44	38	-	20	48	76	-
	10	12	10	7	7	9	-	11	8	6	-

TABLE 12 (CONT.)

THE FOLLOWING IS A LIST OF STATEMENTS ABOUT PEOPLE'S BELIEFS. PEOPLE HAVE A VARIETY OF BELIEFS ON THESE MATTERS SO PLEASE INDICATE WHETHER YOU, PERSONALLY, AGREE OR DISAGREE WITH EACH STATEMENT, NO MATTER WHAT YOU THINK OTHER PEOPLE BELIEVE.	TOTAL	GENDER		AGE GROUPS				NORTH/EAST SCOTLAND	HIGHLANDS & ISLANDS
		MALE	FEMALE	18 TO 24	25 TO 44	45 TO 54	55+		
IF A PERSON IS GENERALLY GOOD, OR DOES ENOUGH GOOD THINGS FOR OTHERS DURING THEIR LIFE, THEY WILL GO TO HEAVEN									
strongly agree	8%	14%	9%	11%	9%	29%	6%	6%	5%
tend to agree	27	24	30	21	34	47	31	23	18
tend to disagree	31	14	11	16	11	13	11	13	12
strongly disagree	9	35	27	37	31	28	31	31	37
don't know	7	20	23	15	25	23	21	27	28
THE SINGLE MOST IMPORTANT PURPOSE OF YOUR LIFE IS TO LOVE GOD WITH ALL YOUR HEART, MIND, SOUL AND STRENGTH									
strongly agree	7%	8%	7%	8%	6%	7%	9%	5%	9%
tend to agree	15	16	15	21	10	13	19	14	9
tend to disagree	23	21	2	47	20	26	26	22	16
strongly disagree	42	44	8	14	47	40	36	39	49
don't know	13	12	14	10	17	15	10	21	18
YOU HAVE MADE A PERSONAL COMMITMENT TO JESUS CHRIST THAT IS STILL IMPORTANT IN YOUR LIFE TODAY									
strongly agree	8%	8%	9%	10%	6%	9%	9%	6%	5%
tend to agree	18	19	16	12	14	16	23	18	19
tend to disagree	21	22	21	23	20	24	21	15	19
strongly disagree	40	42	39	45	43	38	37	42	47
don't know	13	10	16	10	17	13	10	20	16

	REGION						CHRISTIAN ENGAGEMENT				EVANGEL-ICALISM
	SOUTH SCOTLAND	WEST SCOTLAND	CENTRAL	MID-SCOTLAND & FIFE	LOTHIANS	GLASGOW	PRACTISING CHRISTIAN	NON-PRACTISING CHRISTIAN	OTHER FAITHS / NONE (FAVOURABLE)	OTHER FAITHS / NONE (UNFAVOURABLE)	EVANGELICAL
	13%	10%	9%	3%	8%	10%	17%	10%	8%	2%	4%
	33	28	33	34	21	27	48	40	23	7	8
	16	13	11	13	13	9	6	14	12	12	4
	18	28	28	19	39	33	20	16	33	63	80
	20	21	19	21	20	21	9	20	25	15	4
	7%	10%	7%	10%	7%	6%	41%	5%	1%	1%	84%
	15	20	17	13	14	16	39	22	9	1	16
	28	19	23	30	23	22	16	35	24	11	-
	36	37	40	38	50	46	2	24	55	80	-
	15	15	13	9	7	11	3	14	10	7	-
	12%	12%	8%	6%	7%	9%	49%	5%	-%	1%	92%
	25	20	20	18	13	15	42	28	11	-	8
	26	22	24	24	2	20	6	32	25	13	-
	25	32	36	43	49	44	1	22	55	80	-
	13	14	12	10	1	12	3	13	9	6	-

DATA TABLES, NATIONAL STUDY

TABLE 12 (CONT.)

THE FOLLOWING IS A LIST OF STATEMENTS ABOUT PEOPLE'S BELIEFS. PEOPLE HAVE A VARIETY OF BELIEFS ON THESE MATTERS SO PLEASE INDICATE WHETHER YOU, PERSONALLY, AGREE OR DISAGREE WITH EACH STATEMENT, NO MATTER WHAT YOU THINK OTHER PEOPLE BELIEVE.	TOTAL	GENDER		AGE GROUPS				NORTH/EAST SCOTLAND	HIGHLANDS & ISLANDS
		MALE	FEMALE	18 TO 24	25 TO 44	45 TO 54	55+		
WHEN YOU DIE YOU WILL GO TO HEAVEN BECAUSE YOU HAVE CONFESSED YOUR SINS AND ACCEPTED JESUS AS YOUR SAVIOUR									
strongly agree	7%	7%	7%	10%	4%	7%	7%	5%	7%
tend to agree	17	17	16	18	15	15	18	14	11
tend to disagree	18	16	19	12	17	22	18	16	11
strongly disagree	38	40	36	46	39	30	37	37	44
don't know	22	20	23	14	24	26	19	29	28
EVERYONE GOES TO HEAVEN WHEN THEY DIE, BECAUSE GOD LOVES ALL PEOPLE									
strongly agree	4%	4%	4%	6%	3%	2%	5%	5%	2%
tend to agree	16	13	19	19	15	14	17	18	12
tend to disagree	21	22	20	19	19	25	20	16	18
strongly disagree	34	39	30	35	35	33	34	34	35
don't know	25	22	27	21	27	27	23	27	33

	REGION						CHRISTIAN ENGAGEMENT				EVANGEL-ICALISM
	SOUTH SCOTLAND	WEST SCOTLAND	CENTRAL	MID-SCOTLAND & FIFE	LOTHIANS	GLASGOW	PRACTISING CHRISTIAN	NON-PRACTISING CHRISTIAN	OTHER FAITHS / NONE (FAVOURABLE)	OTHER FAITHS / NONE (UNFAVOURABLE)	EVANGELICAL
	8%	9%	5%	7%	7%	5%	40%	15%	1%	1%	76%
	21	23	20	19	11	16	42	25	11	2	24
	23	18	22	20	15	16	10	12	20	10	-
	26	31	34	33	50	41	3	23	47	75	-
	21	19	19	20	18	22	13	23	21	12	-
	7%	7%	4%	5%	4%	3%	14%	4%	4%	1%	-%
	12	15	21	14	11	17	28	23	15	4	-
	34	20	20	26	22	18	29	27	19	11	4
	21	35	33	35	40	35	20	20	34	69	96
	26	23	23	20	23	27	9	26	28	16	-

TABLE 13

WHICH OF THE FOLLOWING WORDS OR PHRASES, IF ANY, DO YOU THINK BEST DESCRIBES YOUR UNDERSTANDING OF JESUS CHRIST?	TOTAL	GENDER		AGE GROUPS				NORTH/EAST SCOTLAND	HIGHLANDS & ISLANDS
		MALE	FEMALE	18 TO 24	25 TO 44	45 TO 54	55+		
was not an actual historical person	7%	6%	9%	12%	9%	4%	5%	6%	7%
speaks to you in a way that is relevant to your life	13	15	12	11	10	13	16	10	11
heals people today	10	11	10	10	8	10	13	9	7
was a person who actually lived, but was just a moral teacher or prophet and not God	37	12	33	32	31	38	43	39	39
is God	12	12	11	10	9	14	14	9	12
is actually returning to earth again	8	9	7	10	6	10	8	7	9
was made out to be the 'Son of God' by his followers after his death	24	24	20	21	21	24	28	27	25
is most concerned with morality and doing good	22	24	19	22	16	24	25	23	23
has deeply transformed your life	8	9	7	7	6	8	10	7	7
his followers are not good examples of his teaching	12	14	10	8	11	14	14	14	12
none of the above	15	12	18	13	17	15	13	19	18
don't know	13	12	14	10	12	13	11	12	16

	REGION						CHRISTIAN ENGAGEMENT				EVANGEL-ICALISM
	SOUTH SCOTLAND	WEST SCOTLAND	CENTRAL	MID-SCOTLAND & FIFE	LOTHIANS	GLASGOW	PRACTISING CHRISTIAN	NON-PRACTISING CHRISTIAN	OTHER FAITHS / NONE (FAVOURABLE)	OTHER FAITHS / NONE (UNFAVOURABLE)	EVANGELICAL
	5%	3%	9%	10%	8%	9%	5%	5%	9%	10%	-%
	13	20	13	11	9	11	0	13	5	1	88
	11	12	10	14	10	10	48	11	3	-	76
	39	33	37	36	40	35	16	36	50	53	4
	10	19	12	8	8	12	55	10	5	1	88
	7	11	6	7	7	8	38	7	1	1	92
	15	26	24	24	27	20	18	25	25	30	12
	28	20	21	16	23	20	39	28	21	7	32
	12	9	7	10	8	7	45	5	3	-	84
	3	10	12	7	13	17	11	12	10	18	24
	15	12	12	26	12	12	3	17	13	7	-
	15	14	13	7	12	613	1	10	11	19	4

TABLE 14

WHICH OF THE FOLLOWING WORDS OR PHRASES, IF ANY, DO YOU THINK DESCRIBES SCOTLAND TODAY?	TOTAL	GENDER		AGE GROUPS				NORTH/EAST SCOTLAND	HIGHLANDS & ISLANDS	
		MALE	FEMALE	18 TO 24	25 TO 44	45 TO 54	55+			
a Christian nation	31%	36%	26%	25%	25%	32%	38%	27%	30%	
a secular nation	19	21	18	22	20	20	18	19	14	
a post-Christian nation	17	20	14	27	15	14	16	17	9	
a nation in transition spiritually	15	17	14	14	15	15	16	15	14	
don't know	23	14	31	22	32	22	16	28	35	
prefer not to say	1	1	1	1	1	1	1	1	2	

	REGION						CHRISTIAN ENGAGEMENT				EVANGEL-ICALISM
	SOUTH SCOTLAND	WEST SCOTLAND	CENTRAL	MID-SCOTLAND & FIFE	LOTHIANS	GLASGOW	PRACTISING CHRISTIAN	NON-PRACTISING CHRISTIAN	OTHER FAITHS / NONE (FAVOURABLE)	OTHER FAITHS / NONE (UNFAVOURABLE)	EVANGELICAL
	49%	30%	33%	35%	28%	28%	39%	47%	24%	13%	8%
	15	18	17	20	23	22	19	13	24	30	40
	7	19	15	17	23	18	19	12	23	26	44
	10	14	17	18	14	17	18	15	18	15	12
	25	21	25	18	18	20	11	19	20	21	8
	-	1	-	1	1	1	-	1	1	1	-

APPENDIX B
DATA TABLES, BEST PRACTICES STUDY

TABLE 1 | LEADER TRAINING & EMPOWERMENT

	GROWING	BASELINE	GROWING	BASELINE
	CHURCH LEADERS		CONGREGATION	
Q: HOW TRUE ARE EACH OF THE FOLLOWING STATEMENTS FOR YOUR CHURCH? (% COMPLETELY TRUE)				
People who are invited to lead in the church must display a godly character, a calling to leadership and be committed to improving as leaders.	57%	18%	---	---
Leadership development is a high priority in our church.	30%	5%	36%	9%
Leadership is exercised through teams, not by individuals.	27%	11%	28%	21%
Church members are encouraged to take on leadership roles in the church.	26%	16%	36%	16%
Church leaders believe that it is better to do a few things with excellence than to do many things poorly.	22%	12%	25%	20%
Every person who regularly attends the church is encouraged to get involved in some type of ministry.	22%	12%	---	--
Constructive criticism is actively sought and received by church leaders, without denial or defensiveness.	17%	9%	18%	12%
The church leadership is decentralised and flexible.	9%	6%	---	---

TABLE 1 | LEADER TRAINING & EMPOWERMENT (CONT.)

	GROWING	BASELINE	GROWING	BASELINE
	CHURCH LEADERS		CONGREGATION	
Q: HAVE YOU, PERSONALLY, EVER RECEIVED LEADERSHIP TRAINING FROM YOUR CHURCH?				
Yes	---	---	39%	34%
No	---	---	61%	66%
Q: HOW WOULD YOU RATE THE LEADERSHIP TRAINING YOU RECEIVED FROM YOUR CHURCH? (% AMONG THOSE WHO ANSWERED YES TO PREVIOUS QUESTION)				
Excellent	---	---	46%	19%
Good	---	---	41%	56%
Adequate	---	---	12%	21%
Poor	---	---	1%	4%

TABLE 2 | LEADER EFFECTIVENESS & ACCOUNTABILITY

	GROWING	BASELINE	GROWING	BASELINE
	CHURCH LEADERS		CONGREGATION	
Q: HOW EFFECTIVE IS YOUR CHURCH LEADERSHIP TEAM?				
Very effective	61%	26%	---	---
Q: HOW TRUE ARE EACH OF THE FOLLOWING STATEMENTS FOR YOU PERSONALLY? (% COMPLETELY TRUE)				
Our church has a team of ministry leaders with complementary leadership skills.	70%	19%	---	---
We make continuous efforts to communicate the vision of the church to the congregation.	48%	19%	---	---
We encourage the congregation to think about the future of the church.	39%	23%	---	---
The church's leaders promote and practise mutual accountability.	39%	14%	---	---
The main standard for evaluating ministries is evidence of positive life transformation.	35%	9%	---	---
A major priority of the church is to train or disciple leaders.	30%	9%	---	---
My ability to lead the church is regularly evaluated by other leaders.	19%	4%	---	---

TABLE 2 | LEADER EFFECTIVENESS & ACCOUNTABILITY (CONT.)

	GROWING	BASELINE	GROWING	BASELINE
	CHURCH LEADERS		**CONGREGATION**	
Q: HOW TRUE ARE EACH OF THE FOLLOWING STATEMENTS FOR YOU PERSONALLY? (% COMPLETELY TRUE)				
Teacher and facilitator training and evaluation are high priorities at the church.	22%	2%	---	---
When an existing ministry cannot show that it is impacting lives, that ministry is closed down without bitterness or significant resistance.	4%	7%	---	---

TABLE 3 | CHURCH COMMUNITY

	GROWING	BASELINE	GROWING	BASELINE
	CHURCH LEADERS		**CONGREGATION**	
Q: HOW TRUE ARE EACH OF THE FOLLOWING STATEMENTS FOR YOUR CHURCH? (% COMPLETELY TRUE)				
My church offers adult and/or family small groups that regularly meet for Bible study, prayer and Christian fellowship.	96%	61%	70%	48%
The church is a safe place for people to explore faith and doubt, and to ask questions.	83%	39%	58%	36%
Building honest and deep relationships with one another is one of the core values of the church.	52%	19%	---	---
The church regularly cooperates in outreach activities with other nearby churches or organisations.	13%	14%	---	---
The church is a place where I belong.	---	---	63%	45%
My faith is encouraged when I am around people from church.	---	---	57%	41%
My church community supports me in difficult times.	---	---	54%	40%
I feel comfortable that my friends who are not Christians would feel welcomed and able to explore faith at this church.	---	---	47%	37%

TABLE 3 | CHURCH COMMUNITY (CONT.)

	GROWING	BASELINE	GROWING	BASELINE
	CHURCH LEADERS		CONGREGATION	
Q: HOW TRUE ARE EACH OF THE FOLLOWING STATEMENTS FOR YOUR CHURCH? (% COMPLETELY TRUE)				
The church has an active and healthy *children's* ministry.	82%	54%	74%	68%
The church has an active and healthy *youth* ministry.	46%	38%	62%	40%
The church has an active and healthy ministry for *young adults*.	27%	23%	42%	40%
The church has an active and healthy ministry for *adults over the age of 60*.	36%	18%	39%	24%
The church has an active and healthy ministry for *families*.	55%	19%	51%	37%

TABLE 4 | THE BIBLE

	GROWING	BASELINE	GROWING	BASELINE
	CHURCH LEADERS		CONGREGATION	
Q: HOW TRUE ARE EACH OF THE FOLLOWING STATEMENTS FOR YOUR CHURCH? (% COMPLETELY TRUE)				
Sermons consistently offer both biblical principles and life application.	83%	57%	62%	34%
We teach the Bible systematically, also known as expository.	83%	8%	---	---
Discipleship, Bible teaching and worship at our church help attenders to develop a biblical worldview.	70%	33%	55%	36%
We use stories and testimonies to illustrate the Bible's teaching.	39%	17%	---	---
Resources such as study guides are provided to encourage the congregation to engage with the Bible on their own.	30%	22%	26%	15%
We teach the Bible by topic, to address current issues and needs.	9%	14%	---	---
Q: HOW TRUE ARE EACH OF THE FOLLOWING STATEMENTS FOR YOUR CHURCH? (% COMPLETELY TRUE)				
The Bible teaching I receive in my church is relevant to my life.	---	---	55%	27%
Attending church has helped me understand the Bible better.	---	---	59%	36%
The Bible contains everything I need to know to live a meaningful life.	---	---	71%	53%

TABLE 4 | THE BIBLE (CONT.)

	GROWING	BASELINE	GROWING	BASELINE
	CHURCH LEADERS		CONGREGATION	
Q: WHAT ARE THE 2-3 MOST SIGNIFICANT WAYS THAT BIBLE TEACHING AND BIBLE ENGAGEMENT IN YOUR CHURCH HAVE HELPED YOU IN THE LAST YEAR, IF ANY?				
Helped you grow closer to God	---	---	62%	45%
Helped you to feel loved by God	---	---	45%	42%
Helped to change your priorities in life	---	---	44%	40%
Helped you feel confident about sharing your faith with others	---	---	34%	26%
Helped to change something about your relationships, such as parenting or marriage or friendships	---	---	29%	30%
Helped you become more knowledgeable about theology	---	---	20%	19%
Helped to transform how you view and use money	---	---	10%	9%
None of these	---	---	6%	14%

TABLE 4 | THE BIBLE (CONT.)

	GROWING	BASELINE	GROWING	BASELINE
	CHURCH LEADERS		CONGREGATION	
Q: IN WHICH SETTING DO YOU, PERSONALLY, FIND THE BIBLE MOST USEFUL? (TICK 1-2 ANSWERS)				
When I hear it preached	---	---	51%	43%
When I discuss it with others	---	---	47%	57%
When I read it alone	---	---	41%	42%
When I face a crisis in my life	---	---	19%	18%
When I have to explain it to others	---	---	17%	13%
None of these	---	---	0%	0%

TABLE 5 | EVANGELISM & OUTREACH

	GROWING	BASELINE	GROWING	BASELINE
	CHURCH LEADERS		CONGREGATION	
Q: HOW TRUE ARE EACH OF THE FOLLOWING STATEMENTS FOR YOUR CHURCH? (% COMPLETELY TRUE)				
The church teaches that evangelism is more than an event.	87%	30%	61%	42%
The congregation is encouraged to talk about their faith in Jesus with others.	78%	37%	63%	47%
Those who are not Christian feel welcome at this church.	65%	19%	38%	28%
Evangelism and discipleship are integrated, not isolated; those who accept Christ are consistently nurtured toward maturity.	48%	9%	---	---
The church sponsors outreach events designed to meet the needs of the local community.	44%	21%	56%	34%
The church provides outreach training.	17%	7%	26%	8%

TABLE 6 | SERVING & SOCIAL JUSTICE

	GROWING	BASELINE	GROWING	BASELINE
	CHURCH LEADERS		**CONGREGATION**	
Q: HOW TRUE ARE EACH OF THE FOLLOWING STATEMENTS FOR YOUR CHURCH? (% COMPLETELY TRUE)				
Serving the needs of people outside the church is equally important to serving the needs of people within the congregation.	41%	14%	48%	24%
There are programmes in place at the church that support people in need in our local community (e.g., the poor, elderly, single mums, widows or families).	27%	11%	40%	25%
The church expands people's comfort zones in outreach or community service.	23%	2%	37%	15%
Q: WHICH TYPES OF OUTWARD ENGAGEMENT AND SERVICE IS YOUR CHURCH INVOLVED IN? (TICK AS MANY AS APPLY)				
Serving local schools	96%	81%	91%	55%
Supporting mission partners overseas	91%	74%	92%	97%
Supporting families	83%	51%	75%	62%
Supporting and helping the elderly	74%	68%	67%	40%
Feeding the poor	57%	88%	69%	82%
Working to address extreme global poverty	57%	42%	52%	46%

TABLE 6 | SERVING & SOCIAL JUSTICE (CONT.)

	GROWING	BASELINE	GROWING	BASELINE
	CHURCH LEADERS		CONGREGATION	
Q: WHICH TYPES OF OUTWARD ENGAGEMENT AND SERVICE IS YOUR CHURCH INVOLVED IN? (TICK AS MANY AS APPLY)				
Addressing justice locally or nationally (such as homelessness and unemployment)	52%	25%	55%	39%
Addressing justice internationally (such as child prostitution, trafficking, racism, sectarianism)	30%	26%	34%	31%
Other	9%	7%	10%	9%
None of the above	0%	0%	0%	0%
Q: IN A TYPICAL MONTH, WHICH TYPES OF OUTWARD ENGAGEMENT AND SERVICE DO YOU, PERSONALLY, ENGAGE IN, WHETHER THROUGH YOUR CHURCH OR OTHERWISE? (TICK AS MANY AS APPLY)				
Supporting families	---	---	40%	28%
Supporting mission partners overseas	---	---	39%	41%
Supporting and helping the elderly	---	---	27%	19%
Feeding the poor	---	---	28%	30%
Addressing justice locally or nationally (such as homelessness and unemployment)	---	---	24%	16%

TABLE 6 | SERVING & SOCIAL JUSTICE (CONT.)

	GROWING	BASELINE	GROWING	BASELINE
	CHURCH LEADERS		CONGREGATION	
Q: IN A TYPICAL MONTH, WHICH TYPES OF OUTWARD ENGAGEMENT AND SERVICE DO YOU, PERSONALLY, ENGAGE IN, WHETHER THROUGH YOUR CHURCH OR OTHERWISE? (TICK AS MANY AS APPLY)				
Serving local schools	---	---	20%	12%
Working to address extreme global poverty	---	---	15%	23%
Addressing justice internationally (such as child prostitution, trafficking, racism, sectarianism)	---	---	13%	12%
Other	---	---	19%	17%
None of the above	---	---	14%	17%
Q: OVERALL, WHICH COMES CLOSEST TO YOUR CHURCH'S PERSPECTIVE ON ENGAGING IN SOCIAL JUSTICE?				
It has been a positive thing for sharing the Gospel.	65%	46%	---	---
It has been neither good nor bad for sharing the Gospel.	13%	19%	---	---
It has been a distraction from sharing the Gospel.	0%	4%	---	---
Not sure	22%	32%	---	---

TABLE 7 | PRAYER & WORSHIP

	GROWING	BASELINE	GROWING	BASELINE
	CHURCH LEADERS		CONGREGATION	
Q: HOW TRUE ARE EACH OF THE FOLLOWING STATEMENTS FOR YOUR CHURCH? (% COMPLETELY TRUE)				
All significant ministry decisions and activities are made prayerfully.	57%	38%	59%	38%
We pray specifically for the challenges of living faithfully in a post-Christian culture.	55%	20%	41%	21%
Listening to God is a widely practised element of prayer.	26%	11%	33%	17%
Prayer does not feel like a formal routine, but a vibrant part of our church life.	17%	14%	38%	16%
Prayer events are held regularly and are well attended.	9%	5%	16%	8%

TABLE 7 | PRAYER & WORSHIP (CONT.)

	GROWING	BASELINE	GROWING	BASELINE
	CHURCH LEADERS		CONGREGATION	
Q: HOW TRUE ARE EACH OF THE FOLLOWING STATEMENTS FOR YOUR CHURCH? (% COMPLETELY TRUE)				
People are regularly reminded that worship is a lifestyle, not just an event.	70%	29%	50%	36%
Church worship services are important to growing an individual's understanding of who God is.	70%	35%	---	---
The worship focus is on connection with God, not on musical performance or sermon brilliance.	44%	27%	46%	35%
Q: WHICH OF THE FOLLOWING TERMS ACCURATELY DESCRIBES THE WORSHIP STYLE OF YOUR CHURCH? (TICK ALL THAT APPLY)				
Modern (such as contemporary music)	87%	79%	83%	85%
Traditional (such as hymns)	48%	58%	40%	35%
Charismatic (that is, believing in the gifts of the spirit)	9%	23%	30%	28%
Liturgical	0%	14%	3%	28%
None of these	0%	5%	3%	2%

TABLE 8 | THEOLOGY & RELIGIOUS ACTIVITY

	GROWING	BASELINE	GROWING	BASELINE
	CHURCH LEADERS		CONGREGATION	
Q: PLEASE READ THE LIST BELOW AND INDICATE WHICH, IF ANY, OF THE FOLLOWING ACTIVITIES YOU HAVE DONE IN THE PAST 30 DAYS.				
Volunteered any of your free time to help your church	---	---	82%	80%
Attended a church small group	---	---	70%	61%
Talked to someone who is not a Christian about my faith	---	---	66%	60%
Volunteered any of your free time to help a ministry, organisation or community group not with your church	---	---	52%	56%
Q: WHEN WAS THE LAST TIME YOU ATTENDED CHURCH, OTHER THAN FOR A HOLIDAY SERVICE, SUCH AS CHRISTMAS OR EASTER, OR FOR SPECIAL EVENTS SUCH AS A WEDDING OR FUNERAL?				
Within the past seven days	---	---	89%	92%
Within the past month	---	---	8%	8%
More than 1 month ago, but within the past 6 months	---	---	2%	1%
More than 6 months ago, but within the past year	---	---	<1%	0%
More than 1 year ago	---	---	<1%	0%
Never	---	---	<1%	0%

TABLE 8 | THEOLOGY & RELIGIOUS ACTIVITY (CONT.)

	GROWING	BASELINE	GROWING	BASELINE
	CHURCH LEADERS		CONGREGATION	
Q: HOW LONG HAVE YOU BEEN ATTENDING THIS CHURCH?				
Less than 6 months	---	---	2%	1%
6 months to 1 year	---	---	1%	3%
1 year to fewer than 2 years	---	---	5%	3%
2 years to fewer than 3 years	---	---	6%	5%
3 years to fewer than 5 years	---	---	8%	9%
5 years to fewer than 8 years	---	---	16%	10%
8 or more years	---	---	62%	70%
Q: HOW OFTEN, IF EVER, DO YOU READ THE BIBLE, NOT INCLUDING TIMES WHEN YOU ARE AT A CHURCH OR CHURCH EVENT?				
Never	---	---	3%	0%
Less than once a year	---	---	0%	0%
Once or twice a year	---	---	<1%	1%
Three or four times a year	---	---	4%	2%
Once a month	---	---	10%	7%
Once a week	---	---	8%	16%
Several times a week	---	---	39%	40%
Every day	---	---	37%	34%

TABLE 8 | THEOLOGY & RELIGIOUS ACTIVITY (CONT.)

	GROWING	BASELINE	GROWING	BASELINE
	CHURCH LEADERS		CONGREGATION	
Q: DID YOU GROW UP ATTENDING A CHRISTIAN CHURCH OR NOT?				
Yes	---	---	80%	75%
No	---	---	20%	25%
Q: BEFORE ATTENDING THIS CHURCH, WERE YOU A REGULAR CHURCH ATTENDER OR NOT?				
Yes	---	---	81%	81%
No	---	---	19%	19%
Q: HAVE YOU EVER MADE A PERSONAL COMMITMENT TO JESUS CHRIST THAT IS STILL IMPORTANT IN YOUR LIFE TODAY?				
Yes	---	---	98%	98%
No	---	---	2%	2%
Q: BELOW ARE SOME STATEMENTS ABOUT PEOPLE'S BELIEFS. PEOPLE HAVE A VARIETY OF BELIEFS ON THESE MATTERS. PLEASE INDICATE WHETHER YOU, PERSONALLY, AGREE OR DISAGREE WITH EACH STATEMENT. (% AGREE STRONGLY)				
There is only one God who exists in three distinct persons: the Father, the Son and the Holy Spirit.	---	---	97%	97%
Your religious faith is very important in your life today.	---	---	93%	93%
Jesus Christ is divine in the sense that he was actually God living among humans.	---	---	93%	95%
The Bible teaches that marriage is only between one man and one woman.	---	---	83%	83%

TABLE 8 | THEOLOGY & RELIGIOUS ACTIVITY (CONT.)

	GROWING	BASELINE	GROWING	BASELINE
	CHURCH LEADERS		**CONGREGATION**	
Q: BELOW ARE SOME STATEMENTS ABOUT PEOPLE'S BELIEFS. PEOPLE HAVE A VARIETY OF BELIEFS ON THESE MATTERS. PLEASE INDICATE WHETHER YOU, PERSONALLY, AGREE OR DISAGREE WITH EACH STATEMENT. (% AGREE STRONGLY)				
The Bible is totally authoritative in all that it teaches.	---	---	80%	72%
You, personally, have a responsibility to tell other people your religious beliefs.	---	---	71%	57%
Q: BELOW ARE SOME STATEMENTS ABOUT PEOPLE'S BELIEFS. PEOPLE HAVE A VARIETY OF BELIEFS ON THESE MATTERS. PLEASE INDICATE WHETHER YOU, PERSONALLY, AGREE OR DISAGREE WITH EACH STATEMENT. (% DISAGREE STRONGLY)				
When he lived on earth, Jesus Christ was human and committed sins, like other people.	---	---	85%	87%
If a person is generally good, or does enough good things for others during their life, they will earn a place in Heaven.	---	---	79%	76%
The devil, or Satan, is not a living being but is a symbol of evil.	---	---	75%	63%

TABLE 8 | THEOLOGY & RELIGIOUS ACTIVITY (CONT.)

	GROWING	BASELINE	GROWING	BASELINE
	CHURCH LEADERS		CONGREGATION	
Q: WHICH OF THE FOLLOWING STATEMENTS COMES CLOSEST TO DESCRIBING WHAT YOU BELIEVE ABOUT THE BIBLE? THE BIBLE IS…				
The actual word of God and should be taken literally, word for word	---	---	13%	12%
The inspired word of God, has no errors, some verses are symbolic	---	---	75%	73%
The inspired word of God, has factual or historical errors	---	---	11%	13%
Not inspired, tells how writers understood the ways and principles of God	---	---	<1%	1%
Just another book of teachings written by men that contains stories and advice	---	---	<1%	1%

TABLE 8 | THEOLOGY & RELIGIOUS ACTIVITY (CONT.)

	GROWING	BASELINE	GROWING	BASELINE
	CHURCH LEADERS		CONGREGATION	
Q: WHICH OF THE FOLLOWING WORDS OR PHRASES, IF ANY, DO YOU THINK BEST DESCRIBES YOUR UNDERSTANDING OF JESUS CHRIST? (TICK ALL THAT APPLY)				
Is God	---	---	96%	92%
Is actually returning to earth someday	---	---	91%	83%
Speaks to me in a way that is relevant to my life	---	---	90%	87%
Has deeply transformed my life	---	---	88%	87%
Heals people today	---	---	82%	82%
Has followers who are not good examples of his teaching	---	---	64%	66%
Was most concerned with morality and doing good	---	---	8%	8%
Was made out to be the 'Son of God' by his followers after his death	---	---	7%	7%
Was not an actual historical person	---	---	1%	1%
Was a person who actually lived, but was just a moral teacher or prophet and not God	---	---	1%	1%
None of these	---	---	0%	0%
Don't know	---	---	<1%	0%

TABLE 8 | THEOLOGY & RELIGIOUS ACTIVITY (CONT.)

	GROWING	BASELINE	GROWING	BASELINE
	CHURCH LEADERS		CONGREGATION	
Q: WHICH ONE OF THESE STATEMENTS BEST DESCRIBES YOUR OWN BELIEF ABOUT WHAT WILL HAPPEN TO YOU AFTER YOU DIE?					
When you die you will go to Heaven because you have tried to obey the Ten Commandments.	---	---	0%	1%
When you die you will go to Heaven because you are basically a good person.	---	---	0%	1%
When you die you will go to Heaven because you have confessed your sins and have accepted Jesus Christ as your saviour.	---	---	95%	93%
When you die you will go to Heaven because God loves all people and will not let them perish.	---	---	1%	1%
When you die you will not go to Heaven.	---	---	0%	0%
You do not know what will happen after you die.	---	---	4%	4%

TABLE 8 | THEOLOGY & RELIGIOUS ACTIVITY (CONT.)

	GROWING	BASELINE	GROWING	BASELINE
	CHURCH LEADERS		CONGREGATION	
BIBLE READERS				
Every day	---	---	37%	34%
Several times a week	---	---	39%	40%
Less often	---	---	24%	26%
BORN AGAIN				
Yes	---	---	93%	90%
No	---	---	7%	10%
FAITH SEGMENTS				
Evangelical	---	---	84%	78%
Non-evangelical born again	---	---	9%	13%
Other	---	---	7%	9%

TABLE 9 | STEWARDSHIP & VOCATION

	GROWING	BASELINE	GROWING	BASELINE
	CHURCH LEADERS		CONGREGATION	
Q: HOW TRUE ARE EACH OF THE FOLLOWING STATEMENTS FOR YOUR CHURCH? (% COMPLETELY TRUE)				
Stewardship in my church is understood to be the appropriate use of all the resources entrusted to us by God.	70%	38%	60%	51%
Leaders teach that one's heart for investing God's resources is more important than giving a specific amount of money.	64%	27%	54%	39%
Q: HOW TRUE ARE EACH OF THE FOLLOWING STATEMENTS FOR YOU, PERSONALLY? (% COMPLETELY TRUE)				
We teach that all work is important to God.	74%	45%	---	---
We try to help attenders understand how to live out their faith in the workplace.	52%	36%	---	---
We help people find fulfilment in their work by putting their God-given talents to use.	35%	25%	---	---
I believe that all of the work I do, whether paid or volunteer, is important to God.	---	---	85%	88%
I find fulfilment in my work because I am able to use my God-given talents.	---	---	43%	37%
The biblical teaching I receive at church is applicable to the issues and challenges I face in the workplace.	---	---	35%	19%

TABLE 9 | STEWARDSHIP & VOCATION (CONT.)

	GROWING	BASELINE	GROWING	BASELINE
	CHURCH LEADERS		CONGREGATION	
Q: HOW TRUE ARE EACH OF THE FOLLOWING STATEMENTS FOR YOU, PERSONALLY? (% COMPLETELY TRUE)				
My church does a good job of helping me understand how to live out my faith in the workplace.	---	---	33%	15%
My faith and my work are two separate parts of my life.	---	---	2%	4%

TABLE 10 | CONGREGATION DEMOGRAPHICS

	GROWING	BASELINE	GROWING	BASELINE
	CHURCH LEADERS		CONGREGATION	
GENDER				
Male	---	---	43%	44%
Female	---	---	57%	56%
CHILDREN IN HOUSEHOLD				
Yes	---	---	34%	28%
No	---	---	67%	73%
MARITAL STATUS				
Married	---	---	80%	71%
Single and have never been married	---	---	14%	20%
Separated	---	---	1%	1%
Divorced	---	---	4%	5%
Living with someone to whom you are not married	---	---	0%	1%
Widowed	---	---	2%	3%
AGE GROUPS				
18 to 30	---	---	14%	15%
31 to 49	---	---	35%	45%
50 to 68	---	---	44%	32%
69 or older	---	---	7%	9%

TABLE 11 | CHURCH LEADER DEMOGRAPHICS

	GROWING	BASELINE	GROWING	BASELINE
	CHURCH LEADERS		CONGREGATION	
Q: WHICH OF THE FOLLOWING BEST DESCRIBES YOUR POSITION AT YOUR CHURCH?				
Full time, paid	43%	13%	---	---
Part time, paid	5%	4%	---	---
Full time, volunteer	5%	4%	---	---
Part time, volunteer	38%	64%	---	---
Other	10%	16%	---	---
Q: HAVE YOU RECEIVED FORMAL THEOLOGICAL TRAINING?				
Yes, graduated	33%	22%	---	---
Yes, did not graduate	10%	4%	---	---
No	57%	75%	---	---
GENDER				
Male	76%	62%	---	---
Female	24%	39%	---	---
YEARS AT THE CHURCH				
Less than 20 years	57%	50%	---	---
20 years or more	43%	50%	---	---

TABLE 11 | CHURCH LEADER DEMOGRAPHICS (CONT.)

	GROWING	BASELINE	GROWING	BASELINE
	CHURCH LEADERS		**CONGREGATION**	
	ANNUAL BUDGET			
Under £150,000	27%	27%	---	---
£150,000 to less than £250,000	27%	61%	---	---
£250,000 or more	46%	12%	---	---

APPENDIX C
BIBLIOGRAPHY OF SECONDARY RESEARCH

In order to provide a backdrop for the new research, Barna conducted a review of existing literature concerning the overall cultural and religious landscape in Scotland. We especially considered how it pertains to young adults. In addition, we considered new Christian movements and thinking that may prove beneficial in seeking future religious and spiritual transformation in this country.

The purpose of this review was to provide a starting point and background for the main portion of the research project. The information gathered in our review was invaluable in providing direction and focus for the research we conducted.

While our review indicated that the Christian church in Scotland finds itself in a difficult place, it also indicated that it is a time of excitement and hope. Scotland is in transition (or has already transitioned) from Christendom to post-Christendom. Christians in Scotland are rethinking how to 'do church' and how to engage with culture in the changing cultural landscape. However we found that while large-scale changes to Scotland's cultural and religious landscapes have resulted in a different religious environment, the current way of doing church in Scotland has not yet adapted to this changing environment.

Bibliography

4Children, 'Make Space: Youth Review', 2007.

ACTS, 'Children within the Church Community': Research undertaken in 2007–2008 for the Children in the Church Community Group of Action of Churches Together in Scotland.

Jacinta Ashworth, Research Matters and Ian Farthing, 'Churchgoing in the UK: A Research Report from Tearfund on Church Attendance in the UK', Tearfund, April 2007.

Bible Society, 'Pass It On: Research Report', 2014, http://www.biblesociety.org.uk/uploads/content/projects/Bible-Society-Report_030214_final_.pdf (accessed January 2015).

Gregory A. Boyd, *The Myth of a Christian Nation* (Grand Rapids, MI: Zondervan, 2007).

Peter Brierley, *Future First: Providing Facts for Forward Planning*, Issue No. 24, December 2012.

Peter Brierley, 'Introduction: UK Christianity 2005–2015', originally published in *Church Statistics*, 2011.

Peter Brierley, 'Generations of Older People', originally published in *Church Statistics*, 2011.

Church of Scotland, 'Growing Up in Scotland Today', 2009.

ComRes, 'The Influence of the Bible', for Bible Society, April 2011, http://comres.co.uk/polls/Bible_Society_Tables_April_2011.pdf (accessed January 2015).

John Drane and Olive Fleming Drane, 'Reformed, Reforming, Emerging, and Experimenting: Background to Emerging Church & Fresh Expressions', Joint Working Party of the Ministries Council and the Mission and Discipleship Council, Church of Scotland, 2010.

Evangelical Alliance, 'What Kind of Nation?: Manifesto for a Future Scotland', 2014.

Thomas L. Friedman, *The World Is Flat: A Brief History of the Twenty-First Century* (Philadelphia, PA: Farrar, Straus, and Giroux, 2005).

Fergus McDonald, 'Engaging the Scriptures: The Challenge to Recover Biblical Literacy', *Scottish Bulletin of Evangelical Theology*, Vol. 27, No. 2, Autumn 2009.

Mission and Discipleship Council of the Church of Scotland, 'Future Focus: A Way Forward for Congregations', presented to the General Assembly in 2008.

Mission-Shaped Church Working Group, *Mission-Shaped Church: Church Planting and Fresh Expressions of Church in a Changing Context* (London: Church House Publishing, 2004).

Stuart Murray, *Post-Christendom: Church and Mission in a Strange New World* (Milton Keynes, UK: Authentic Media/Paternoster, 2004).

National Council for Voluntary Youth Services, 'Youth Report 2013', http://www.ncvys.org.uk/publications/youth-report-2013 (accessed January 2015).

National Council for Voluntary Youth Services, 'Youth Report 2014', http://www.ncvys.org.uk/media/186 (accessed January 2015).

Robert D. Putnam, *Bowling Alone: The Collapse and Revival of American Community* (New York: Simon & Schuster, 2000).

Special Commission anent Review and Reform of the Church of Scotland, 'A Church Without Walls', presented to the General Assembly in 2001.

YouthLink Scotland, 'Being Young in Scotland 2007: A Survey of the Hopes, Fears and Aspirations of Over 2,500 Young People Aged 11–25', 2007.

APPENDIX D
METHODOLOGIES

The data contained in this report originated through a series of research studies conducted by Barna Global, the international partner of Barna Group of Ventura, California, USA. The study was commissioned by the Transforming Scotland Steering Group and the Maclellan Foundation.

The full project was completed in multiple stages. To begin, the Barna research team conducted a review of previous research and analysis on ministry and mission in Scotland (see Appendix C).

Next, in-depth interviews were conducted with key leaders of churches and ministries, as well as lay leaders, 14 April to 10 June 2014. A Barna Global representative conducted a total of 29 live interviews: 11 with church leaders, 18 with 'strategic thinkers' (lay leaders). Participants represented a diversity of theological and denominational backgrounds; an array of geographies; and widely varying churches, ministries, businesses and political affiliations. Lay leaders were identified by the Steering Committee and selected based on solid church networks and unique sense of mission. The interviews were recorded with the permission of interviewees and transcribed for analysis.

Following the in-depth interviews, an online survey was conducted among 200 Protestant ministers/pastors from across the nation. Ministry leaders consisted of 46 per cent Church of Scotland, 14 per cent Baptist, 10 per cent Scottish Episcopal, 7 per cent Free Church of Scotland and 23 per cent other.

CHURCH LEADER DEMOGRAPHICS	PROTESTANT PASTORS
GENDER	
male	87%
female	14%
POSITION AT CHURCH	
full time, paid	86%
part time, paid	9%
full time, volunteer	1%
part time, volunteer	3%
other	1%

CHURCH LEADER DEMOGRAPHICS	PROTESTANT PASTORS
YEARS AT THE CHURCH	
1 to 5 years	34%
6 to 10 years	29%
11 or more	37%
ANNUAL BUDGET	
under £75,000	51%
£75,000 or more	49%

A sample list was generated by Transforming Scotland ministry partners, including CLAN, Scottish Baptist Society and the Free Church of Scotland, each of which provided church and leader names and email addresses. Approximately 2,300 churches were contacted via email from 2–11 June 2014 to participate in the study. Of these, 200 completed a survey.

Concurrent with the ministry leader survey, a nationwide study of Scottish adults ages 18 and older was conducted by ComRes using an online panel. Surveys for this portion of the research study were completed 9–16 June 2014. A total of 1,019 surveys were completed. The sample error on this survey is plus or minus 3.1 per cent points at the 95-per cent confidence level. Data were weighted by age, gender and socio-economic grade to be representative of all Scottish adults aged 18 and older.

From 1 December 2014 through 20 January 2015, two online surveys were conducted among Protestant evangelical church leaders and congregations.

Two lists of churches, identified as either 'baseline' or 'growing', were generated by the Steering Group, who formulated these cohorts based on their familiarity with the Scottish church landscape and on widespread perceptions among the evangelical community of churches that demonstrate extraordinary growth. Baseline churches, experiencing limited numerical growth, represent the norm among evangelical churches in Scotland, acting as the 'control group' for the comparison study. Growing churches report significant levels of growth. Because spiritual transformation is a difficult reality to measure, numerical growth—specifically, conversion growth, rather than transfer growth—is a quantitative proxy measurement that often indicates transformative ministry.

From each church, all church leaders, including paid staff and volunteer leaders, were invited to complete the leader survey. A single point of contact then forwarded a survey link to their church leadership and congregations (members and regular attendees) either via email, social networks or other channels, such as the Sunday bulletin or weekly newsletter.

A total of 13 churches participated in the church leader study, including five growing churches and eight baseline churches. The final sample includes 23 surveys completed by church leaders from a growing church and 57 surveys completed by church leaders from a baseline church. Baseline and growing church leaders completed identical surveys about their church operations, perspectives and behaviours—thus enabling parallel comparison. The sample error on this survey is plus or minus 10.8 per cent points at the 95-per cent confidence level.

Ministry leaders consisted of 15 ministers, 7 church staff and 61 elders or other leadership not on staff.

CHURCH LEADER DEMOGRAPHICS	GROWING	BASELINE
GENDER		
male	76%	62%
female	24%	39%
AGE GROUPS		
minimum age	22	17
maximum age	71	84
POSITION AT CHURCH		
full time, paid	43%	13%
part time, paid	5%	4%
full time, volunteer	5%	4%
part time, volunteer	38%	64%

CHURCH LEADER DEMOGRAPHICS	GROWING	BASELINE
POSITION AT CHURCH (CONT.)		
other	10%	16%
YEARS AT THE CHURCH		
less than 20 years	57%	50%
20 years or more	43%	50%
ANNUAL BUDGET		
under £150,000	43%	13%
£150,000 to less than £250,000	5%	4%
£250,000 or more	5%	4%

Fifteen churches participated in the congregation study, including seven growing churches and eight baseline churches. From growing churches, there were 231 completed surveys. From baseline churches there were 154 completed surveys. Baseline and growing church members/attendees completed identical surveys about their beliefs, perspectives and behaviours—thus enabling parallel comparison. Additionally, approximately half of the questions were identical to the church leader study; again, enabling comparison. The sample error for the congregation study is plus or minus 4.7 per cent points at the 95-per cent confidence level.

CONGREGATION DEMOGRAPHICS	GROWING	BASELINE
GENDER		
male	43%	44%
female	57%	56%
AGE GROUPS		
minimum age	20	16
maximum age	80	81

CONGREGATION DEMOGRAPHICS	GROWING	BASELINE
MARITAL STATUS		
married	80%	71%
single and have never been married	14%	20%
separated	1%	1%
divorced	4%	5%
living with someone to whom you are not married	0%	1%
or widowed	2%	3%

CONGREGATION RESPONDENTS	GROWING	BASELINE
Q: HOW LONG HAVE YOU BEEN ATTENDING THIS CHURCH?		
less than 6 months	2%	1%
6 months to 1 year	1%	3%
1 year to fewer than 2 years	5%	3%
2 years to fewer than 3 years	6%	5%

CONGREGATION DEMOGRAPHICS	GROWING	BASELINE
3 years to fewer than 5 years	8%	9%
5 years to fewer than 8 years	16%	10%
8 or more years	62%	70%

Concurrent with the launch of the best practices study (13 December 2014 through 29 January 2015), the researchers commenced a study of Scottish Millennials, ages 18 to 28, involved in congregations and parachurch ministries. The research generated 25 additional completes (male 36%, female 64%), which, when merged with the existing dataset, yielded 103 completed responses from Millennials. This study employed both qualitative and quantitative research methods in an online survey.

APPENDIX E
ACKNOWLEDGEMENTS

The researchers would like to express their appreciation to the Transforming Scotland Steering Group, which includes Andy Bathgate, Elaine Duncan, Neil MacMillan, Alan McWilliam and Ruth Walker, and previous member Mark Ellis.

The project was made possible by the generosity of the Maclellan Foundation of Chattanooga, Tennessee, and the Barna team wishes to thank Scott Maclellan, Charlie Phillips, David Denmark and Pat MacMillan.

The Transforming Scotland research was conducted by Barna Global, UK, and was aided by the efforts of Gareth Russell, Traci Hochmuth, Aly Hawkins, Megan Pritchett, Pam Jacob, Roxanne Stone, Brooke Hempell, Joshua Hook, Rick Ifland and David Kinnaman. Others at Barna—Elaine Klautzsch, Bill Denzel, Joyce Chui, Inga Dahlstedt and Robert Jewe—and the team at Bread PR in Aberdeen helped to produce this monograph and the events surrounding its release.

Many thanks also to Chaz Russo, who designed the *Transforming Scotland* report and all of the infographics.

ABOUT BARNA

Barna Group is a research firm dedicated to providing actionable insights on faith and culture with a particular focus on the Christian church. In its 30-year history, Barna Group has conducted more than one million interviews in the course of hundreds of studies, and has become a go-to source for organizations that want to better understand a complex and changing world.

Our clients include a broad range of academic institutions, churches, non-profits, and businesses, such as Alpha, the Templeton Foundation, Pepperdine University, Fuller Seminary, the Bill and Melinda Gates Foundation, the Maclellan Foundation, DreamWorks Animation, Focus Features, Habitat for Humanity, NBC-Universal, the ONE Campaign, Paramount Pictures, the Salvation Army, Walden Media, Sony and World Vision.

The firm's studies are frequently quoted by major media outlets such as *The Economist*, BBC, CNN, *USA Today*, the *Wall Street Journal*, Fox News, Huffington Post, *The New York Times* and the *Los Angeles Times*.

Barna Group's work reaches around the world through the efforts of **Barna Global**. Current Barna Global projects include engagements in Scotland, England, Australia and South Africa.

Learn more about Barna Group at www.barna.org.